JAPAN GUIDEBOOK

英語で発信！
JAPANガイドブック

英訳日対

【編者】神田外語大学日本研究所
The Research Institute for Japanese Studies,
Kanda University of International Studies

神田外語大学出版局

刊行にあたって

　神田外語大学は、国際的に活躍する若者を輩出する大学を目指し「言葉は世界をつなぐ平和の礎」を理念として1987年に創立されました。日本人の学生は、まず外国語を修得することで諸外国に対する関心を持ち、海外からの留学生は日本語を学ぶことによって日本を知り、お互いの興味を深めあう空間を作ります。日本人学生と留学生が、英語で日本のことを学ぶ授業も開講されています。

　多様な若者が集まり化学反応を起こし新しい価値観を探っています。

　皆様は日本人が当然知っていると思う日本の歴史、文化、社会構造などを何かの機会に英語で説明しようとして思わず詰まったことはありませんか？　また、常識と思い込んでいる習慣の背景を質問され返答に窮したことはありませんか？

　自己を客観視することは容易ではありません。他人から指摘されて自分の長所や短所が分かるように、外国人から日本のことを質問されると日本の素晴らしさや困った面に気付くことがあります。知らないことが沢山あることに気付き、様々な疑問が湧いてきます。また、英語で表現すると新鮮に思えることもあります。神田外語大学「日本研究所」は1992年に設立され日本の文化や歴史、思想、美術などを専門とする日本人と外国人の教員チームが、グローバルな観点から共同で研究、教育に当たり日本を考え議論を深化させております。そのチームで日本を説明

刊行にあたって

　する切り口を纏めたのが、『英語で発信！JAPANガイドブック』です。

　ビジネス、留学や旅行で出会う人たちから聴かれそうな事柄を日本語と英語で出来るだけ簡潔にまとめました。通勤通学の時間に目次だけでも目を通してください。キャンパスで出会う留学生たちと会うのが待ち遠しくなります。出張や旅先での会話が楽しくなります。

　海外へお出かけの際はパスポートと一緒にお持ちください。

2018年4月

神田外語大学学長
宮 内 孝 久

まえがき

　『英語で発信！JAPANガイドブック』は、日本のことについて、英語で説明するための本としてつくられました。左ページに日本語による解説が、右ページにそれに対応した英語による解説が書かれています。

　しかし、いまやこうした本はめずらしくありません。では、本書の特徴は、どこにあるのでしょうか。

　1つめは、取り上げたテーマです。日本について総合的に説明できるようにすることをめざしました。日本の自然、伝統、文化、芸術、精神、歴史などまでをカバーしています。

　現在の日本に関する説明にも力を入れ、近現代の項目を充実させました。海外での人気が高いアニメやアイドルなどのクールジャパンはもちろん、政治、外交、経済、教育なども扱い、日本が直面している問題や課題も取り上げました。

　ですから、読者の中には、英語でどう言ったらよいのかということ以前に、日本語で書かれている内容もよく知らなかったという方もいるかもしれません。

　2つめは、神田外語大学の日本研究所が編集したということです。同研究所には、日本に関する様々な分野を専門とする日本人・外国人の教員が所属し、ふだんからグローバルな雰囲気のなかで活動しています。各教員にはその専門を生かして、項目を執筆してもらいました。

　日本人教員が書いたものは、外国人教員が英訳を担当してい

ます。英文は日本文の直訳ではなく、内容を踏まえたうえで、より英語としてふさわしい表現になっています。日英いずれの項目についても、末尾に担当者の名前を入れました。

　3つめは構成です。目次を見てください。各章は、それぞれのテーマに関する概説と6個のキーワードから構成されています。キーワードは3個ずつをひとまとまりとし、そのまとまりごとに象徴的な漢字（またはアルファベット）1文字を付しました。こうすることで、簡潔な記述に努めつつも、単なる用語集にならないように工夫をしています。

　けれども、本書の評価は読者の皆さんにどのように使ってもらえるかにかかっています。本書を読み、外国人に日本のことについて英語で話してみようという気持ちになり、実際に行動に移してくれればうれしいです。そして、皆さんが、さらに自分自身で調べ、考え、発信できる人になれるように願っています。

　本書の趣旨をご理解くださり、写真のご提供をいただいた方々のおかげで、本書はより魅力的なものとなりました。厚く御礼を申し上げます。

　　　2018年4月

　　　　　　　　　　　　　　　神田外語大学日本研究所所長
　　　　　　　　　　　　　　　　　土　田　宏　成

■目 次■

刊行にあたって／iii
まえがき／v
本書の構成／xi

1 **日本の地形と自然**（Terrain and Nature in Japan） …………… 3
　【姿】（日本の国土、日本の気候、日本の人口）／4
　【遺】（富士山、屋久島、小笠原諸島）／8
　●地図からとらえる日本の形～ヨーロッパは日本をどのように知ったか～／12

2 **日本の年中行事**（Japan's Annual Events） ………………… 15
　【伝】（正月、春分・秋分、盂蘭盆）／16
　【行】（節分、花見、七五三）／20
　●日本の伝統行事／24

3 **伝統と生活**（Tradition and Lifestyle） …………………… 27
　【和】（和食、茶道、和歌）／28
　【術】（柔道、剣道、空手）／32
　●生活の中の伝統芸術と工芸／36

4 **自然との共生**（Coexisting with Nature） ………………… 39
　【災】（関東大震災、阪神・淡路大震災、東日本大震災）／40
　【真】（農業、共生、安藤昌益）／44
　●自然と災害／48

5 **日本人の心**（A Japanese Sense of Self） ………………… 51
　【心】（朱子学、国学、水戸学）／52
　【自】（自分、精神、母性）／56
　●現代社会で働く独身女性の世界観／60

6 **宗教と日本人**（Religion and the Japanese People） …………… 63

【信】（神道、仏教、儒教）／64
　　　【仏】（密教、浄土教、禅宗）／68
　　　●心のルーツを探る／72

7　歴史の中の人と都市（People and Cities in History）………… 75
　　　【人】（公家、武士、忍者）／76
　　　【都】（奈良、京都、江戸）／80
　　　●日本の都市とコミュニティの歴史／84

8　文字文化の変遷（Transitions in Written Culture）………… 87
　　　【字】（漢字、カタカナ、平仮名）／88
　　　【遊】（書道、いろはかるた、『百人一首』）／92
　　　●前後縦横〜日本語の姿〜／96

9　文学にみる日本（Japan as Seen through Its Literature）…… 99
　　　【創】（川端康成、大江健三郎、村上春樹）／100
　　　【継】（源氏物語、おくの細道、坊ちゃん）／104
　　　●翻訳を通して世界から見た日本／108

10　芸術と感性（Art and Sensibility）……………………………… 111
　　　【雅】（やまと絵、絵巻、琳派）／112
　　　【音】（雅楽、アイドル、ビジュアル系）／116
　　　●ジャポニスム／120

11　クールジャパンの系譜（A Genealogy of Cool Japan）………… 123
　　　【C】（AKB48、ヤンキー、ファッション）／124
　　　【楽】（手塚治虫、スタジオジブリ、オタク）／128
　　　●海外におけるアニメと「クールジャパン」の誕生／132

12　西洋との出会い（Encountering the West）…………………… 135
　　　【開】（出島、洋学、留学生）／136
　　　【初】（切支丹、宣教師、『日本大文典』）／140
　　　●明治維新から150年〜近代日本のスタートを知る〜／144

13　近代教育の始まり（The Beginning of Modern Education）…… 147
　　　【学】（学校制度、お雇い外国人、寺子屋）／148

【外】（シーボルト、ヘボン、アーネスト・サトウ）／152
　　　●江戸時代の外国との交流／156
14　近現代の歩み（The Course of Modernity）･･････････････159
　　　【戦】（日清戦争／日露戦争、第一次世界大戦、日中戦争／第二次世界大戦）／160
　　　【国】（天皇、沖縄、アイヌ（先住民族））／164
　　　●アイヌから見た日本社会とは／168
15　近現代の日本経済
　　　（The Modern and Contemporary Japanese Economy）････171
　　　【企】（財閥、総合商社、トヨタ生産方式）／172
　　　【経】（産業革命、高度成長、バブル経済）／176
　　　●GDPの算出方法と日本の現状／180
16　現代日本の政治（Politics in Contemporary Japan）･･････････183
　　　【統】（日本国憲法、内閣制度、地方制度）／184
　　　【議】（国会、選挙、政党）／188
　　　●戦後日本の政治と外交／192
17　現代日本の外交・安全保障
　　　（Foreign Policy and Security in Contemporary Japan）････195
　　　【安】（自衛隊、日米同盟、国際連合）／196
　　　【隣】（日中、日韓、日露）／200
18　個人と家族（Individual and Family）･････････････････205
　　　【家】（家族、既婚／未婚、育児）／206
　　　【若】（一人前、引きこもり、フリーター）／210
　　　●日本人的対人コミュニケーションの根底にある日本文化／214
19　教育の諸相（Aspects of Education）･･･････････････217
　　　【問】（いじめ、教育格差、入学試験）／218
　　　【形】（英語教育、ゆとり教育、日本の大学）／222
　　　●教育の昔・今・これから／226
20　現代社会の課題（Challenges for Contemporary Society）････229

【労】（終身雇用制、過労死、公害）／230
【生】（少子化、限界集落、地域再生）／234
●ビジネスから見る日本近現代史／238

執筆者一覧／241

●コラム　日本の世界文化遺産・無形文化遺産*

❶法隆寺地域の仏教建造物／14
❷姫路城／26
❸古都京都の文化財／38
❹白川郷・五箇山の合掌造り集落／50
❺広島平和記念碑（原爆ドーム）／62
❻嚴島神社／74
❼古都奈良の文化財／86
❽日光の社寺／98
❾琉球王国のグスク及び関連遺産群／110
❿紀伊山地の霊場と参詣道／122
⓫石見銀山遺跡とその文化的景観／134
⓬平泉／146
⓭富士山／158
⓮富岡製糸場と絹産業遺産群／170
⓯明治日本の産業革命遺産／182
⓰ル・コルビュジエの建築作品／194
⓱結城紬*／204
⓲壬生の花田植*／216
⓳那智の田楽*／228
⓴山・鉾・屋台行事*／240

■本書の構成■

【章】日本の文化や歴史、政治や経済、自然や社会といった広い分野から20のテーマを設定しました。

【節】各章には、そのテーマを象徴する漢字（またはアルファベット）1文字を、2つずつ選びました。

【キーワード】各節には、それぞれ3つのキーワードを取り上げて詳解しました。

【エッセイ】テーマによっては、より深い理解のために、エッセイを加えました。

【英訳】本文には対訳として英語をつけました。

【コラム】世界に向けて日本を発信する観点から、各章末に、日本の世界文化遺産と本文に触れられていないいくつかの無形文化遺産を紹介しました。①〜⑮は、公益社団法人日本ユネスコ協会連盟のホームページを、⑯〜⑳は、文化庁や文化遺産が登録されている自治体のホームページなどを参考に編者がまとめました。

英語で発信!
JAPANガイドブック

日本の地形と自然

Terrain and Nature in Japan

【日本の国土】

　日本の国土の面積は、外務省のホームページによると約37万8000km²で、ロシアは日本の約45倍、中国は約26倍、アメリカは約25倍もあります。ドイツ、ベトナム、イラクなどが日本と同じくらいの大きさの国です。

　なお、日本の領海や排他的経済水域の面積は約447万km²と、日本の国土の約12倍の広さがあり、世界第6位です。また、7000近い島々がありますが、住民が住んでいるのは僅か5％未満の島にすぎません。

　国土の大部分を占めるのは、北海道、本州、四国、九州の4つの大きな島です。面積の比率は、四国：九州：北海道：本州＝1：2：4：12となります。

　日本は、およそ東経120度から150度、北緯20度から45度の間にあり、北東から南西へ全長3500kmにわたります。国土の約70％は山地と森林で、14％が農地、居住地はたったの4％に止まります。

　日本は地震が多く、マグニチュード5.0の地震が全世界の10％、マグニチュード6.0以上の地震が全世界の20％、日本周辺で発生しています。

【日本の気候】

　日本の国土は、ほぼ温帯に属しており、四季の区別が明確です。夏は南東から、冬は北西からの季節風の影響を受けて、夏は太平洋側で雨が多く、冬は日本海側で雪が多く降りやすくなっています。

　日本列島は南北に伸びていることと、季節風や海流の影響を受けることから、地域ごとに気候が大きく異なります。北海道は亜寒帯に属し、冬の寒さが厳しく、梅雨はありません。一方、沖縄は亜熱帯に属

The Japanese territory

According to the website of the Ministry of Foreign Affairs, the surface of the Japanese territory is about 378,000 km^2, which is 45 times smaller than Russia, 26 times smaller than the China, and 25 times smaller than United States. It is about the same surface area of countries such as Germany, Vietnam, or Iraq.

On the other hand, the surface of Japan's territorial waters and exclusive economic zones is of about 4,470,000 km^2, twelve times bigger than the land surface, making it the 6th largest in the world. Japan has approximately 7,000 islands, but merely a fraction of 5 % of them are inhabited.

The largest portion of the territory is represented by the four big islands of Hokkaidō, Honshū, Shikoku and Kyūshū. The proportion between the surface of the islands is Shikoku : Kyūshū : Hokkaidō : Honshū = 1 : 2 : 4 : 12.

Japan is situated between the meridians 120 and 150 east, and between the parallels 20 and 45 north, stretching from North-East to South-West over 3,500 km. 70% of the territory is covered by mountains and forests, 14% is agricultural land, and only 4 % is used as residential land.

Japan is an earthquake-prone country, and 10% of tremors with a magnitude of 5.0, and 20% of tremors with a magnitude of or over 6.0 in the entire world occur in the area around Japan.

The climate of Japan

Most of the Japanese territory is situated in the temperate climate zone, and there are clear differences between the four seasons. Under the influence of seasonal winds blowing from the Southeast in summer and from the Northwest in winter, in summer it rains a lot on the Pacific side, whereas in winter it snows a lot on the Sea of Japan side.

Since the Japanese archipelago stretches from North to South and is under the influence of seasonal winds and marine currents, there are big differences in climate between the various regions. Hokkaidō, for example, is situated in the subarctic climate zone, so winters there are extremely cold and there is no rainy season. On the other hand, Okinawa is located

しているため、一年中気温が高いです。

特色と言えるのが、梅雨と台風です。梅雨は6月上旬から7月下旬にかけて降り続ける長雨で、これは梅雨前線が日本列島の南部に停滞するためです。台風は7月から10月にかけて多く通過します。北上する間に強風と集中豪雨をもたらすので、山崩れや高潮、水害などの災害を多く発生させます。

近年は地球温暖化による、高温・豪雨といった異常気象が各地で頻繁に起こっており、自然災害への注意が必要となり、生態系への影響も危惧されます。

関東・東北豪雨で発生した水害（2015.9／茨城県）(写真提供：時事)

【日本の人口】

日本の総人口（2016年）は、約1億2700万人で、世界第10位です。その約70％は、東京から北九州にかけての温暖な太平洋岸の地域に集中しています。

1960年以降、都市とその周辺への人口集中が始まり、東京・名古屋・大阪の三大都市圏に約43％が居住しています。また、関東地方に約32％が集中しており、地方の過疎化は大きな問題となっています。

65歳以上の高齢者人口（2015年）は約3400万人、総人口に占める65歳以上人口の割合（高齢化率）は26.7％と極めて高い数値です。一方で出生数は約100万人で、女性が一生に産む子どもの平均数・合計特殊出生率（2012年）は、1.41と深刻な少子化です。

また、平均寿命は男性81歳、女性は87歳で過去最高を更新、世界でも有数な「長寿社会」となっています。日本はOECD諸国の中で、最も少子高齢化が激しく、世界のどの国も経験したことのない速度で人口の少子化・高齢化が進行しています。

（町田明広）

in the subtropical climate zone, which means that the temperature is relatively high all year round.

The rainy season (*tsuyu*) and typhoons might be considered two characteristics of the Japanese climate. *Tsuyu* usually lasts from the beginning of June to the end of July, and it comes with almost uninterrupted rains caused by a stationary front in the southern part of the Japanese archipelago. Typhoons usually occur from July through October. As they move northward, they bring strong winds and heavy rainfall, often causing damages such as landslides or floods.

In recent years, due to the intensification of global warming, unusual weather phenomena such as extremely high temperatures and cloudbursts have become more frequent. These are considered to be warning signs that indicate the extent of the damage to the ecosystem, as well as a wake-up call to the magnitude of natural disasters.

The population of Japan

The population of Japan was of approximately 127,000,000 people in 2016, making it the 10th most populated country in the world. About 70% of the population is concentrated on the Pacific Ocean side, which has a milder climate, on a strip extending from Tokyo to Northern Kyūshū.

In the 1960s, people began to concentrate in and around the big urban centers, and now 43% of the population lives in the three cities of Tokyo, Osaka and Nagoya. Moreover, 32% of the population is concentrated in the Kantō area, which makes the depopulation of the other regions a serious problem.

The number of people aged over 65 in 2015 was of approximately 34,000,000, meaning that the proportion of senior citizens is 26.7%, which represents an extremely high figure. The number of births was approximately 1,000,000 and, given that the average number of children a woman gives birth to is 1.41 (in 2012), it is clear that the declining birthrate is a severe problem.

The average life expectancy has reached new record levels of 81 years for men and 87 years for women, making Japan one of the few "long-living societies" in the world. Japan has the worst declining birthrate among all OECD countries, and it is becoming an aging society at a pace that no other country in the world has experienced. (Tr. R. Paşca)

【富士山】

　富士山は標高3776m、日本最高峰の独立峰です。静岡県と山梨県にまたがる活火山であり、日本の象徴として知られています。富士山についてのもっとも古い記録は奈良時代に編纂された『常陸国風土記』にあるとされ、その表記は「福慈岳(ふじたけ)」です。

　「富士の風や扇にのせて江戸土産」という、芭蕉の俳句にもあるように、富士山は日本人にとって昔から親しみやすい存在であり、信仰の対象でもあります。その風貌は数多くの作品の題材とされ、芸術面でも大きな影響を与えてきました。葛飾北斎が描いた『富嶽三十六景』の浮世絵はその代表的な例の1つです。

　2013年に「富士山〜信仰の対象と芸術の源泉」としてユネスコの世界文化遺産リストに登録されて以来、訪れる国内外の観光客の数が一気に増えました。しかし一方で、観光客の増加に伴いゴミやタバコの吸い殻のポイ捨て問題が深刻化しています。富士山を保護しながらその美しい自然をどう楽しむかが大きな課題になってきています。

【屋久島】

　屋久島は九州の南60kmぐらいの海上に位置し、鹿児島県では奄美大島に次いで2番目に大きい島です。1993年に姫路城、法隆寺、白神山地とともに日本で初めて世界遺産リストに登録されました。

　面積は約505km^{2}ですが、その90%が森林で覆われています。日本国内で積雪が観測される最南端であり、様々な植物相や動物相が存在しています。中

屋久杉（写真提供：公益財団法人屋久島観光協会）

Mount Fuji

Standing at 3776 m, Mount Fuji is the tallest peak in Japan. Well known as a symbol of Japan, it is an active volcano which straddles the boundary between Shizuoka and Yamanashi prefectures. The oldest mention of the mountain — as "Fujitake" — is found in an old chronicle called *Hitachi no kuni fudoki*, compiled in the Nara period.

As can be seen in Bashō's *haiku* "the wind of Mt. Fuji / I brought it on my fan / a souvenir from Edo," for the Japanese people Mount Fuji has been a familiar presence and an object of worship since the ancient times. It has served as inspiration for numerous works, and it has exerted a great influence in Japanese art. One of the most representative examples is Katsushika Hokusai's series of woodblock prints titled "Thirty-six Views of Mount Fuji."

Since 2013, when the mountain was added by UNESCO to the Cultural World Heritage Sites List as "Fujisan, sacred place and source of artistic inspiration," the number of tourists has increased dramatically. This increase has triggered a serious garbage problem, with large quantities of trash and cigarette butts being discarded on the mountain. How to protect the mountain while enjoying the beauty of nature is an issue that needs to be addressed immediately.

Yakushima

Located about 60 km south of Kyūshū, Yakushima is the second largest island in Kagoshima prefecture after Amami Ōshima. In 1993, it was part of the first group of places in Japan to be added to the UNESCO Natural World Heritage Sites List, along with the Buddhist Monuments in the Horyu-ji Area, Himeji-jo, and Shirakami-Sanchi.

The surface of the island is about 505 km^2, and 90% of it is covered by forests. It is the southernmost point in Japan where snowfalls are recorded, and it is home to a very diverse

でも、小型のヤクシカなどの動物と屋久杉が特に有名です。「縄文杉」と呼ばれている杉の樹齢は、2000年以上と推定されています。

屋久島は様々な作品に登場し、白谷雲水峡「苔むす森」は宮﨑駿監督の映画『もののけ姫』の舞台イメージのモデルの1つでもあります。

ここ数年、観光客の激増により登山道の劣化、設備整備の遅れ、ゴミ処理などが社会的問題になり、自然環境との共生と資源の保護を考え、入島料やエコツーリズムなどの解決策が検討されています。

白谷雲水峡「苔むす森」
（写真提供：公益財団法人屋久島観光協会）

【小笠原諸島】

小笠原諸島は東京より約1000km南、太平洋上にある30余の島々であり、東京都の管轄下にあります。江戸時代には「無人島」と呼ばれていました。1972年に国立公園に指定され、2011年に世界遺産リストに登録されました。

小笠原諸島の特徴としては、総面積がやや小さいことと、他の陸地から大きく離れていることが挙げられます。これらの特徴は生物相の形成に大きく関与し、それぞれの島々の生態系では独自の進化を遂げた固有種が数多く分布しています。その特徴としては、例えば雌雄異株である植物の割合が高いこと、そして草食動物が存在しなかったため有毒な植物が極めて少ないことなどです。

一方、開発による自然環境の破壊が深刻な問題になってきています。そのため、一部の島々が立ち入り制限区域とされたり、一日の上陸者数が制限されたりなど、様々な対策が施されています。

小笠原諸島の1つ母島　小富士からの眺望
（写真提供：小笠原村観光局）

ムニンヒメツバキ（小笠原諸島の固有種）（写真提供：小笠原村観光局）

（ロマン・パシュカ）

ecosystem. Yakushima is known especially for the *yakushika*, a variety of sika deer, and for the *yakusugi*, a variety of Japanese cedar. The oldest tree on the island is said to be the *Jōmon sugi*, whose age has been estimated to over 2000 years.

Yakushima has appeared in numerous works of art — for example, the Shiratani Unsuikyo Ravine — inspired the scenery featured in director Hayao Miyazaki's *Princess Mononoke*.

In recent years, due to the increasing number of visitors, the degradation of mountain roads, the lack of facilities, and garbage processing have become serious social problems. At present, various measures are being considered in order to protect the environment and preserve the natural resources, including implementing a tax for visitors and promoting ecotourism.

The Ogasawara Islands

The Ogasawara archipelago is a group of some thirty islands located in the Pacific Ocean about 1,000 km south of Tokyo. The islands are under the jurisdiction of the Tokyo metropolitan government. During the Edo period, they were called Bunin ("uninhabited"). In 1972 they were designated as a National Park, and later in 2011 they were added to the Natural World Heritage Sites List.

Two of the characteristics of the Ogasawara islands are the relatively small surface, and the fact that they are located at a great distance from any continent. These characteristics have had a great impact on the flora and the fauna, as on each island there developed a unique ecosystem, with many indigenous species. For example, the proportion of dioecious plants is very high, and there are extremely few species of poisonous plants as there were no herbivores living on the islands.

Development of the islands in the modern period has also brought about destruction of the natural environment. In order to prevent further damage, measures have been put in place to forbid access to some of the islands, and to limit the number of visitors on others. (R. Paşca)

地図からとらえる日本の形
～ヨーロッパは日本をどのように知ったか～

　ヨーロッパに日本を最初に紹介したのは、14世紀以降、広く読まれたマルコ・ポーロの『東方見聞録』でした。日本を、「黄金の国ジパング」として紹介しました。その姿は15世紀の地図上にようやく現われましたが、当時は誰一人として日本を見たわけではなく、黄金郷への憧れが地図の上に描かせたのでしょう。

　大航海時代のポルトガル人の種子島漂着（1543年）によって、日本の実在が知られると、1550年代には地図作家と言われる職業人が日本を描き始めました。例えば、「ミュンスター南北アメリカ大陸図」では、アメリカ大陸の西に巨大なジパング島が描かれ、「7448の群島」という記載は『東方見聞録』から採ったものです。

　16世紀後半には、日本図が次々と描かれました。中でも、当時ヨーロッパで人気の地図帳『世界の舞台』の中で様々な形で多数描かれたため、日本は多くの人々に認知されることになりました。なお、日本図の刊行はアジアの方が先んじており、最古版日本図は李氏朝鮮で1402年に完成しています。

　ヨーロッパにおける地図の歴史を見ると、アジア東北部、つまり日本列島周辺地域の地図化が最後までできずに残されました。ヨーロッパから見て、「極東」の地である日本列島の地図化は遅れ、特に北海道ならびにその北方地域は厳しい自然環境よって、世界地図の上で最後まで"未知の領域"として残されていました。

　19世紀前半、ようやく日本列島の正しい姿がヨーロッパにもたらされました。それは、シーボルトが国禁を犯して持ち出した、伊能忠敬の『大日本沿海輿地全図』のお蔭です。伊能図は、シーボルトが日本研究を集大成した『日本』の中にありました。念願の正しい日本図をヨーロッパは手に入れましたが、ジパングからの日本像変遷の旅は、およそ400年にも及んだことになります。（町田明広）

Japan seen through its maps
~ How did Europe find out about Japan? ~

The first text that introduced Japan to Europeans was *The Travels of Marco Polo*, which was widely read from the 14th century onward. Japan was mentioned as Zipangu, the land of treasures. Its shape started to appear on maps in the 15th century, even though at the time nobody had actually been in person in Japan, so it was rather the illustration of an El Dorado they were longing for.

In the 1550s, after the existence of Japan was known firsthand in 1543 when a Portuguese ship drifted ashore in Tanegashima during the Age of Discoveries, cartographers started to draw maps of Japan. For example, in "Münster's map of North and South America," a giant island called Zipangu is depicted West of the American continent, accompanied by the inscription "archipelago of 7448 islands", taken from Marco Polo's text.

Various maps of Japan were drawn in the second half of the 16th century. Among them, the maps included in the popular atlas *Theatrum Orbis Terrarum* which circulated in Europe made Japan known to a large number of people. But the first detailed maps of Japan were published in Asia, the oldest one being completed in 1402 in Korea by Yi Hoe.

If we examine the history of maps in Europe, we see that the cartography of the Northeastern part of Asia including the Japanese archipelago and its surroundings was never completed. Seen from Europe, Japan is situated in the "Far East," and so its mapping was delayed; Hokkaidō and all territories situated to the North, where the climate is unfavorable, were left until the end as "unknown lands" on world maps.

Japan's correct shape finally became known to Europe in the first half of the 19th century through Inō Tadataka's *Dai Nihon Enkai Yochi Zenzu* ("Maps of Japan's coastal Areas"), which was brought by Philipp von Siebold, who broke the law in order to take it out of Japan. Inō's map was included in Siebold's book entitled *Nippon*, a comprehensive work that contained the results of his years of research in Japan. Thus, Europe finally had access to the true image of Japan it had hoped for, but the journey from Zipangu took approximately 400 years.   (Tr. R. Paşca)

❖日本の世界文化遺産❖

法隆寺地域の仏教建造物
Buddhist Monuments in the Horyu-ji Area

《世界最古の木造建造物群》

　この遺産には、法隆寺の建造物47棟と法起寺の三重塔を加えた48棟が含まれ、全て国宝あるいは重要文化財の指定を受けています。そのうち7世紀末から8世紀にかけて造られた11棟は、現存する世界最古の木造建造物の1つとして高く評価されました。中でも法隆寺の金堂、五重塔、中門、回廊は、中国・朝鮮にも残存しない初期の仏教木造建築の様式をもっています。

【所在地】奈良県　【登録年】1993年
【写　真】法隆寺（提供：株式会社便利堂）

② 日本の年中行事
Japan's Annual Events

【正月】

　正月は、本来、旧暦の1月の別名でした。1873年に太陽暦が導入されてから、現在の1月1日から始まる1か月が正月となり、元旦は祝日となっています。正月に行われる慣習には色々ありますが、基本的には家族が集まって、新年を無事に迎えられたことを祝う時となっています。

　大晦日にはNHKの紅白歌合戦などの特別番組を家族で見て、寛いだ時間を過ごし、お正月には寺社に初詣に行きます。また賀詞に旧年中の感謝と変わらぬ厚誼をお願いする言葉を述べた年賀状を、知人・友人・顧客らに送ります。子どもにはお年玉を渡します。

　正月に関係する食べ物もたくさんあります。蒸したもち米を杵でついて作るお餅もそうですが、伝統的なお正月料理といえば「おせち」です。おせちの起源は平安時代にまで遡ります。長寿を象徴するもの、また健康や幸運などを願う縁起物の料理が主で、めでたさが重なるように重箱に詰めて出されることが多いです。

おせち（写真提供：株式会社紀文食品）

【春分・秋分】

　春分とは、昼と夜の長さがほとんど同じになる3月下旬の一日で、年によって日が異なります。また日本以外でも多くの国で春の始まりと理解されています。同じように9月にある秋分の日は、秋の始まりを意味します。春分・秋分を中日とした数日間は「彼岸」と呼ばれますが、これは仏教の教えに基づいています。

　古代から春分や秋分は先祖を供養する日であり、墓参りをして花や食べ物を墓に供えてきました。しか

Japanese New Year

The Japanese New Year used to be celebrated on the first day of the Chinese lunar calendar, but from 1873 with the adoption of the Gregorian calendar it was moved to January 1st. The first several days of the New Year are a holiday, and while there are various activities, fundamentally it is a time for families to come together and celebrate.

In addition to customary temple or shrine visits, families relax at home and enjoy television specials, such as NHK's *Red & White Song Competition* (*Kōhaku Uta Gassen*), broadcast on New Year's Eve. Other New Year activities include New Year's Day postcards (*nengajō*), sent to friends, acquaintances, and clients to show appreciation for the past year, and New Year's Day money (*otoshidama*), given in special envelopes to children.

There are many foods traditionally associated with New Year celebrations. Rice cakes (*mochi*), made by pounding sticky rice with a big mallet, are one customary food. Traditional New Year's foods (*osechi*) are often combined and served in a box (*jūbako*), a tradition dating from the Heian period. Many of the seasonal foods represent longevity, health, and other positive qualities that are believed to be enhanced by stacking them in a box.

Equinox

In Japan, as with many countries, spring is customarily believed to begin with the vernal equinox (*shunbun*) in March, and autumn with the autumnal equinox (*shūbun*) in September. These are times when day and night are of approximately equal length, and the date varies depending on the year. The time around an equinox is called *higan*, a term with ancient Buddhist origins.

Since ancient times, the vernal and autumn equinoxes were times to show respect to one's ancestors. People would visit family graves to clean them and make offerings of flowers or food. In modern times, the days have been turned into secular

し、現代ではこうした信仰はうすれ、単なる休日の意味合いが強くなっています。春分は春の始まりにふさわしく桜の花が開花し始める時でもあり、自然の美しさを称え、五穀豊穣を願う時期です。また、学年暦の終わりとも一致します。

秋分の日は収穫に感謝し、季節の変わり目を迎えて寒い冬が訪れる前に、家族で行楽に出かけたりして屋外での時間を楽しむ時期となっています。また、寺社でのお祭りが多く行われる時期でもあります。

【盂蘭盆】

盂蘭盆会（お盆）は、日本の夏の年中行事で最も大切なものです。死後の先祖の苦しみを和らげるという仏教の教えが基ですが、今は先祖を供養する行事となっています。太陽暦が採用されてから8月半ばの3日間に行われることが多くなりましたが、旧暦の日付に合わせて7月半ばに行う地域もあります。

この時期に先祖の霊が子孫の元へ戻ってくると信じられているため、その霊をお迎えするために故郷へ帰省する人も多いです。お盆の初日には迎え火を焚き、先祖の霊を家へ迎え入れます。

お盆の行事の中で最も有名なのが、盆踊りです。元々先祖の霊を迎える宗教的な意味を有していました。地域によって踊りや音楽は異なりますが、長く続く地域文化に深く根差したものです。徳島県の阿波踊りなどはとても有名で、多くの観光客が訪れます。お盆が終わると、送り火で先祖の霊をもう一度送り出しますが、灯篭流しと言って海や川などに流す場合もあります。

（亀井ダイチ・アンドリュー）

holidays. Vernal Equinox Day, befitting the onset of spring, is a time to celebrate nature and agriculture, particularly the beautiful cherry blossoms that start to bloom around this time. It also coincides with the end of the school year.

Autumnal Equinox Day is a time to give thanks for the harvest and enjoy being outside before colder days begin. Families may take short trips and reconnect with relatives. It is also a time for many festivals at shrines and temples.

Obon Festival

The Obon Festival is one of the most important Japanese traditional summer events. A Buddhist custom, it evolved from a concern with alleviating the suffering of ancestors to a holiday to remember them and show appreciation. The festival is three days long, and while most of Japan celebrates it in mid-August, some regions, in line with the old lunar calendar, do so in mid-July.

Because the spirits of the ancestors are believed to come and visit their descendants at this time, it is important for many people to travel to their hometowns so as to be ready to greet them. Welcoming fires (*mukaebi*) are set out on the first day to guide the spirits to their homes.

The most famous aspect of the festival is the traditional dances (*Bon odori*). These dances, which evolved from religious performances to welcome the spirits, vary greatly in style and music depending on location. Many dances are deeply-rooted in local culture and date back centuries. Some, like Tokushima's *Awa Odori*, are very famous and draw large numbers of tourists. When the festival ends, families send the spirits off by once again using fires (*okuribi*), in some locales sending them out to sea or down a river (*tōrōnagashi*).

(A. T. Kamei-Dyche)

【節分】

節分とは、もともと季節が分かれる節目の日という意味で1年に4回ありましたが、次第に2月初めに行われるもののみを意味するようになりました。

節分には「鬼は外、福は内」と言いながら、炒った豆をまき、年齢の数だけ豆を食べて厄除けをします。家族の誰かが鬼のお面をかぶって鬼の役をすることもあります。この鬼というのは、日本の昔話によく出てくる妖怪の一種のようなものですが、鬼が登場するのは、季節の変わり目には邪気が生じ、人間の世界と魔の世界との境目が揺らぐからという考え方に基づいています。

今では子どもを中心に家族全員で豆まきをしますが、本来は家の主人かその年の干支の生まれの人のみでした。その他に、柊(ひいらぎ)の小枝に焼いたイワシの頭を玄関先に飾ったりします。また近年では、太巻きを切らないまま、その年の恵方(えほう)に向いてかぶりついて食べる「恵方巻」の風習も全国に広まっています。

【花見】

花見とは、文字通り「花を見る」という意味です。

花見自体は奈良時代からありましたが、当時は梅が主流で、「花見」が桜を意味するようになるのは平安時代初期からです。元々は上流社会のみの行事でしたが、近世に入る頃には庶民の間にも広がり、春の娯楽としての地位を確立しました。

桜の開花時期は日本社会において大切なニュースで、毎年その開花予想が発表されます。同じ日に開花予想をされた地域を線で結んだものを、桜前線と

Setsubun

Setsubun originally referred to a day that divided two seasons. There were therefore four *Setsubun* each year. However, gradually "*Setsubun*" came to mean only the spring *Setsubun* in early February.

On *Setsubun*, Japanese families take roasted soybeans and throw them outside the front door, or at a family member wearing an *oni* mask. While doing this, they say, "*Oni wa soto! Fuku wa uchi!*" (Demons out! Fortune in!). This custom, called *mamemaki* (bean scattering), represents purifying the home from negative forces. People also eat one soybean for each year of their age.

Oni, the demon- or ogre-like creatures from Japanese folklore, have long been associated with *Setsubun* because of the belief that during seasonal change negative forces are unleashed and the borders of the human world and the spirit world weaken.

Nowadays it is more common for the whole family to perform *mamemaki* with children being the focus, but originally it was considered best if it was performed by the head of the household or a person born in a year of the same zodiac symbol as the current year. Another custom is to affix cooked sardine heads on a sprig of *hiiragi* outside their door. Recently, the custom of *ehōmaki*, where people eat large uncut sushi rolls while looking in the direction deemed to be fortunate for the year, has also spread around Japan.

Hanami

Hanami ("flower viewing") refers to the traditional seasonal practice of going to sit under cherry blossom trees and enjoy their beauty. This dates back to the Nara period when it was more common to view plum blossoms, but by the early Heian period *hanami* was firmly associated with cherry blossoms. While originally an elite event, by the early modern era it had become a popular seasonal activity for common people as well.

The blooming of the trees is an important news item and is forecast every year. Locales where the blooming occurs on the same day are connected by a line called the "Cherry Blossom Front." Because the flowers are only in bloom for several days, they represent transient beauty, an appreciation of which is

呼びます。桜が開花してから散るまでの期間は数日間と短いのですが、その儚さこそが、「もののあはれ」を象徴するものとして、長年親しまれてきました。

現代では、桜が花開く時期になるとその花の下に集まり、飲み食いを楽しみながら花見をする人が多く見られます。桜のある公園などは、花見の場所取りをする花見客で非常に混雑します。夜に花見をする場合は「夜桜」と呼ばれますが、こうして夜に花を愛でるのは桜独特の慣習です。

【七五三】

七五三の記念写真

七五三は、子どもの健やかな成長を祝う行事です。地域にもよりますが、11月15日に3歳7歳の女子、また3歳5歳の男子が主に神社にお参りをします。七五三の年齢は、古代東アジアの文化では奇数がラッキーナンバーだと考えられていたことからだと言われています。

七五三の発祥は、平安時代に公卿たちの間で行われていた類似の儀式と言われています。それが武士階級にも広まり、明治時代には一般庶民の間でも行われるようになりました。今日でも七五三の時に子どもに着物を着せることが多いですが、これは男児は5歳で初めて袴を身につけ、また女児は7歳で着物を着る際に大人と同じ帯を締め始めるという慣習の一部が引き継がれたものです。祝い方は地方によっても多少異なりますが、一般的には家族で神社に参拝し、お祓いをし、祝詞をあげてもらい、記念写真を撮ります。また、七五三には千歳飴がつきものですが、これは色が縁起の良い紅白で、形が細長いことから、子どもの健康と長寿を願う気持ちが込められています。

（亀井ダイチ・アンドリュー）

called *mono no aware* and is an element of Japanese aesthetics.

In contemporary society, Japanese often gather to hold parties under the cherry blossoms, enjoying food and drink. Parks with cherry blossoms become crowded with people, who stake out a spot for their group. When this occurs at night, it is called *yozakura* (night cherry blossoms), and enjoying the beauty of flowers at night is normally only done with cherry blossoms.

Shichi-go-san

Shichi-go-san is a seasonal event wishing for the healthy growth of children. While there is regional variation, it usually occurs on November 15, and is a traditional rite of passage for three- and seven-year-old girls and three- and five-year-old boys. These ages are believed to have come from the idea that in classical East Asian thought odd numbers are lucky.

Shichi-go-san likely developed from ceremonies conducted by the court nobility in the Heian period. It later spread among samurai families and by the Meiji period came to be practiced by commoners as well.

Traditionally, this rite of passage was marked by changes in clothing. Boys who had turned five would start to wear *hakama*, and girls who had turned seven would start to tie their kimono with an *obi*. Today, during *Shichi-go-san* children of the relevant ages and genders will usually put on a kimono for the first time. How it is celebrated varies by region, but generally the children's families take them to a shrine to purify them and pray for a long and healthy life for them. A commemorative photo is often taken. Children may also eat *chitose ame* (thousand-year candy), which are long red and white sweets representing wishes for health and longevity.

(A. T. Kamei-Dyche)

日本の伝統行事

　年中行事とは毎年決まって行われる行事や儀式のことで、私たちの暮らしに深く根付いています。年中行事の発祥の時期や理由は様々で、正月、節分、彼岸、月見などの季節に基づいたものや、七五三や成人式など年齢や人生の節目を祝うもの、お盆など先祖供養をするもの、勤労感謝の日のもととなった新嘗祭など、農耕と関連するものがあります。こうした年中行事を行う日を「ハレ（非日常）」の日と呼び、日常を意味する「ケ」の日と区別します。

　こうした年中行事の中には毎年同じ日に行われるものもあれば、年によって異なる場合もあり、その大半は法律で定められた祝日ではありません。しかし近代にその発祥をもつこどもの日や海の日、山の日、敬老の日などは国民の祝日となっています。

　ある特定の年中行事や季節に結びついている食べ物も色々あります。正月のおせち料理や土用丑の日の鰻、冬至のカボチャ、大晦日の蕎麦などがそうした例として挙げられます。年中行事の中にはクリスマスやハロウィーン、バレンタインデーなど海外から入ってきた行事もあり、既に日本の文化の一部として定着しています。しかし、元々はイエス・キリストの生誕を祝う宗教行事としてキリスト教圏では家族が集まるクリスマスが日本では恋人同士のイベントとなったり、女性が男性にチョコなどの贈り物をして愛を告白する日として日本では理解されているバレンタインデーなど、商業化されたものも多いです。3月14日のホワイトデーは、そうした商業化のなかで作り出された行事の代表的な例と言えるでしょう。

　時代が経つにつれて年中行事のやり方は変わりつつありますが、そこに込められた思いは、現代社会にも引き継がれています。

　　　　　　　　　　　　　　　　　（亀井ダイチ・アンドリュー）

Annual Events in Japan

Annual events (*nenchū gyōji*) are events or ceremonies that are carried out at certain times every year. These events are deeply rooted in Japanese culture and are part of daily life.

The origins of annual events, and how the events developed over time, are varied. Some are based on the seasons, such as New Year's, *Setsubun*, *Higan*, and *Otsukimi*; some are based on celebrating rites of passage, such as *Shichi-go-san* and *Seijin-shiki* (coming-of-age ceremonies) ; some are based on showing respect for one's ancestors, such as *Obon*; and some are related to agriculture, such as *Niinamesai* (first fruit festival), which became the origin of Labor Thanksgiving Day. Days with special events are known as *hare no hi* (auspicious days) while regular days are called *ke no hi* (inauspicious days).

Some annual events are conducted on the same day every year, while others vary. Most are not official national holidays. National holidays, most of which are of modern origin, include Children's Day, Sea Day, Mountain Day, and Respect for the Aged Day.

Various foods are often associated with particular annual events or seasons: for example, *osechi-ryōri* with New Year's, *unagi* with the midsummer Day of the Ox (*Doyo no ushi no hi*), pumpkins with the winter solstice, and soba with New Year's Eve.

Among annual events are some that were imported from overseas, such as Christmas, Hallowe'en, and Valentine's Day, which have also become part of Japanese culture. However, the meaning of these events has changed, and they are often commercialized. For example, Christmas, which in Christian countries originated as a religious event to honor the birth of Jesus Christ and is a time for families to come together, is in Japan an event for couples, while Valentine's Day is understood to be a day when women confess their love to men through gifts such as chocolate. White Day, on March 14, could be said to be a representative example of an annual event artificially produced by commercialization.

As time passes, how annual events are celebrated changes, but the essence, such as respecting nature or other people, endures and these events continue to have a role in contemporary society.

(A. T. Kamei-Dyche)

❖日本の世界文化遺産❖

姫路城
Himeji-jo

《美しさと機能性を兼ねそなえた近代城郭》

　城の形が優美で壁などに白い漆喰（しっくい）を使っていることから、昔は白鷺城（しらさぎ）とも呼ばれてきた姫路城は、独特な城郭の造りをもつ17世紀初めの日本の城郭を代表するものです。14世紀に建てられた城が関ヶ原の戦いの後に大改修され、江戸城に次ぐ規模になりました。城郭内部の建築構造は、この大改修時のまま残っており、周辺地域とともに保全されています。

【所在地】兵庫県　【登録年】1993年
【写　真】姫路城（提供：姫路市）

伝統と生活
Tradition and Lifestyle

和食の基本形
「一汁三菜」

【和食】

「和食」という言葉からイメージされる料理は色々ありますが、その基本形は「一汁三菜」と言えるでしょう。汁物一種におかず三種（主菜一種、副菜二種）、そこにご飯、香の物の組み合わせで構成される献立です。一汁三菜は、その栄養バランスの良さと繊細な味付けから、世界中で人気が高まってきている日本型食生活です。

日本の料理は、魚だけではなく貝や甲殻類などの魚介類を多く使います。また「ダシ」をとり、そこからうま味成分（酸味・甘味・塩味・苦味の四味に加えられた第五の基本味）をとりだし、それぞれの食材の持ち味を引き立てるのが、その特徴の1つです。自然をうまく取り入れ、目にも美しい形に仕上げることも重要視されます。

ファーストフードなどの普及による衰退が懸念されていましたが、2013年には「和食 日本人の伝統的な食文化」はユネスコ無形文化遺産に登録され、和食はその良さが見直されることになりました。

【茶道】

抹茶と和菓子

茶道とは茶の湯ともいい、抹茶を用いて茶を点て、それを振る舞う伝統的な様式です。お茶を飲む習慣は平安時代に中国からもたらされました。当初は仏教寺院等を中心に行われているだけでしたが、日本国内で茶の栽培が普及するにつれ他の社会層にも普及しました。

16世紀には千利休によって簡素簡略を重んじる「わび茶」の様式が完成して、茶道は1つの芸術として

Japanese Cuisine

A classic staple of Japanese cuisine is *ichijū san-sai*, or "one soup, three dishes." This type of set meal includes soup, a main dish, and two side dishes, and is served along with rice and pickled vegetables. *Ichijū san-sai* is gaining popularity around the world for its subtle taste and good nutritional balance.

In addition to seasonal vegetables, Japanese cooking makes extensive use of seafood, including not only a great variety of fish, but also shellfish and crustaceans. Another common element in much cuisine is *dashi* (Japanese broth), encapsulating umami (a taste distinct from sour, bitter, salty and sweet). Great emphasis is placed on a natural style and presenting dishes with a pleasing appearance.

While there were concerns about the decline of traditional Japanese cuisine due to fast food, the UNESCO recognition of *washoku* as an Intangible Cultural Heritage in 2013 brought it renewed attention.

Tea Ceremony

The Japanese tea ceremony is a traditional form of preparing and serving fine powdered green tea (*matcha*). The tradition of enjoying this type of tea in ritual fashion was introduced from China during the Heian period, and soon spread among Buddhist institutions.

It then expanded among other social classes, and reached a new level of sophistication under tea master Sen no Rikyū in the 16th century.

Ideally, a tea ceremony should be performed in a dedicated tea room with tatami flooring and a *tokonoma* (decorative alcove).

のレベルに達することになります。

　茶道は、畳敷きで床の間のある茶室で行われるのを最善とし、その場を含め、茶碗に始まる茶杓や茶筅などの茶道具も重要な要素となります。和菓子や懐石が提供される場合もあります。

　茶道の点前の所作は、無駄のない、流れるような美しい一連の動きによって成り立っていますが、その所作は流派によって異なります。茶道は、文化的な趣味の1つとして、現在でも比較的高い人気を誇っています。また京都の宇治市は、抹茶の生産地として有名です。

【和歌】

　和歌は日本の古典詩の一分類です。和歌という言葉は、古典中国語で書かれた漢詩に対する日本語の詩を意味するものとして発生したと言われています。

　五音と七音の句を組み合わせてできており、良く知られている形式として短歌（五七五七七）と長歌（五七を3回以上繰り返して七音で終わる）があります。現在「和歌」といえば、短歌を指すのが一般的です。

　現存最古の和歌集は万葉集（759年頃）で、相聞歌・雑歌・挽歌の三種類の和歌が4500首程収められています。平安時代から中世初期にかけて、多くの勅撰和歌集が編まれました。

　また中世には、和歌の韻律を基盤として複数人で連作する「連歌」が生まれています。連歌の発句のうち卑俗性・滑稽性が高いものが近代になって独立して発展した文学形式が「俳句」です。

（亀井ダイチ・アンドリュー）

Specialized tools include such things as *chashaku* (tea scoop), *chasen* (tea whisk), and *chawan* (tea bowl). Along with the actual tea, sweets and/or a light meal may be served.

The precise sequence of events making up a ceremony is highly formalized but varies from school to school. Tea ceremony remains one of the more popular traditional cultural pastimes. The city of Uji in Kyoto Prefecture is particularly known for its *matcha*.

Waka

Waka refers to a genre of classical Japanese poetry. Unlike *kanshi*, which were written in a form of classical Chinese, *waka* were in Japanese. *Waka* consisted of combinations of lines of 5 and 7 syllables per line, and the two most common types of poem were *tanka* (5-7-5-7-7) and *chōka* (5-7-5-7-5-7... with a final 7 ending line). *Tanka* became so common that they eclipsed all other types and became synonymous with *waka*.

The oldest extant *waka* anthology is the *Man'yōshū* (c. 759), containing some 4,500 poems of three main types (*sōmonka*, *zōka*, and *banka*). Later during the Heian through early medieval periods, a series of anthologies were compiled at royal command.

The medieval era witnessed the birth of *renga* (linked verse, meaning poetic sequences) which in turn paved the way for the comic opening verse tradition that eventually became *haiku* in early modern times.

(A. T. Kamei-Dyche)

【柔道】

嘉納治五郎師範
（取材協力：公益財団法人講道館）

　柔道は1882年に嘉納治五郎が創始した近代武道であり、1964年以来、オリンピックの種目にもなっています。天神真楊流柔術や起倒流柔術という江戸時代の古流派から発展した武道で、投げ技、固め技、捨身技などを中心とした技法を持っています。

　嘉納は、「精力善用」「自他共栄」または「柔よく剛を制す」といった原理を重視し、かつての武術とは異なる、近代化が進む新しい時代にふさわしい技術と理論を組み立てました。彼は自己完成を目指す「道」として柔道を構想しました。柔道の最初の道場にその道を講ずるところという意味で「講道館」という名前をつけました。

　柔道の稽古には、「乱取り」と「形」という2つの方法があります。乱取りは自由な方法で練習することで、形はあらかじめ順序と方法を決めて練習し、柔道の技法の原理を学びます。

【剣道】

　剣道は剣術を競技化した武道です。江戸時代中期の直心影流剣術の長沼国郷がいち早く竹刀と防具を使用した打ち込み稽古を導入したと言われています。江戸時代末期に流派を超えて広く試合が行われるようになり、明治時代には大日本武徳会が試合規則を定めました。1911年に中等学校正科の一部として採用されることによって「剣道」という名称が定着し、競技として成立しました。

　第二次世界大戦の敗戦により大日本武徳会は戦争遂行に加担したとして解散させられ、剣道も禁止され

Judo

Judo is a form of modern *budō* (martial way) founded by Kanō Jigorō in 1882 and, since 1964, it has been included as an Olympic sport. It was developed from the Edo-period Tenjin Shinyō Ryū (Divine True Willow School) and Kitō Ryū (Rise and Fall School) schools of *jujutsu* and its techniques center around *nage-waza* (throwing techniques), *katame-waza* (grappling techniques) and *sutemi-waza* (sacrifice techniques).

Kanō envisioned Judo as a "way" (*michi*) of self-completion, different from the *bujutsu* martial arts of the past. He saw Judo as an ensemble of technique and theory, suitable for a new modernizing age, and emphasized the principles of *senryoku senyō* (maximum efficient use of power), *jita kyōei* (mutual prosperity for self and others), and *jū yoku gō wo seisu* (flexibility overcomes brute force). He chose the name Kōdōkan for the first Judo *dōjō*, meaning a place where the way is taught.

Judo practice consists of *randori* (free-style practice) and *kata* (forms in which the order and method of techniques are decided in advance), from which the principles of Judo can be learnt.

Kendo

Kendo is a competitive form of *budō* (martial way) developed from older forms of *kenjutsu* (swordsmanship). It is said that Naganuma Kunisato of the Kashima Shinden Jikishinkage-Ryū (Divinely Transmitted, Honest Reflection of the Heart School) school of *kenjutsu*, first introduced competitive *uchikomi* training using *shinai* (bamboo sword) and *bōgu* (training armor) in the mid-Edo period. Toward the end of the Edo period, competitions were being widely held regardless of specific *kenjutsu* school and, in the Meiji period, the Dai Nippon Butoku Kai (Greater Japan Martial Virtue Society) set down the first collective competitive rules. The name "Kendo" became common after the practice was incorporated into the junior high school national curriculum in 1911.

After the defeat in the Second World War, the Dai Nippon

ました。しかし、サンフランシスコ講和条約後、全日本剣道連盟が結成され、復興が始まりました。全日本剣道連盟は1975年に剣道の理念を「剣の理法の修練による人間形成の道である」と定めました。

現在、剣道は世界中に普及し、剣道家の人口は600万人と言われています。剣道の稽古は、竹刀と防具を使用する竹刀稽古と木刀、模擬刀、刃引(はびき)で行う形稽古に大別されています。

【空手】

空手は琉球王国時代の沖縄に発祥した武道です。空手のルーツは、琉球王国の中級士族である親雲上(ペーチン)によって伝承された沖縄固有の拳法「手」(ティー)もしくは唐手(トーディー)と中国(主に福建省由来の)武術が加味されて発展してきたことにあると言われています。今日の空手道は主に近代において発展したもので、打撃技を主体とした格闘技として知られていますが、沖縄系流派は様々であり、関節技や投げ技、さらに棒術、釵術(さいじゅつ)、ヌンチャク、トンファー、櫂(ウェーク)などを含む琉球古武術と共に稽古が行われます。

近代空手道が誕生したのは、昭和初期に摩文仁(まぶに)賢和(けんわ)(糸東流(しとう))、宮城長順(ちょうじゅん)(剛柔流)、船越義珍(ぎちん)(松濤館(しょうとうかん))らが本土で稽古の指導に当たり、1933年に大日本武徳会から日本の武道として認められたことからでした。船越が『般若心経』の「空」の概念から唐手を空手に改めると発表したのをきっかけに「空手」という表記が広まりました。

(マーク・ウィンチェスター)

船越義珍
(写真提供:日本空手道松濤會)

Butoku Kai was disbanded due to its collaboration with Japan's war effort and the practice of Kendo was banned. However, after the signing of the San Francisco Peace Treaty, the All Japan Kendo Federation was founded and Kendo began to be practiced officially once again. In 1975, the All Japan Kendo Federation established that Kendo should be "a way to discipline the human character through the application of the principles of the katana (sword)."

Today, Kendo is practiced around the world and it is said that there are up to 6 million active practitioners. Kendo practice consists of *shinai-keiko* (practice using the bamboo sword and training armor) and *kata-keiko* (practice using wooden swords and blunted training blades.)

Karate

Karate is a form of *budō* (martial way) that originates from Okinawa and the days of the Ryūkyū Kingdom. The roots of Karate are in the combination of an old indigenous Okinawan martial art practiced by the Pechin scholar-official class of the Ryūkyū Kingdom known as *ti* (hand), or *todi* (Tang hand), and Chinese martial arts, particularly those coming from the Fujian province of southeast China. The Karate-dō of today developed mainly in the modern era and is known as a martial art based upon striking techniques. However, there are many different Okinawan styles of Karate, some of which include joint locking and throwing techniques, and they are often practiced alongside other traditional Ryūkyūan martial arts such as *bōjutsu* (staff techniques), *saijutsu* (sai techniques), *nunchaku, tonfa, eku* (oar), and others.

Modern Karate-dō was born after Mabuni Kenwa (Shito-Ryū), Miyagi Chōjun (Gōjū-Ryū) and Funakoshi Gichin (Shōtōkan) began to teach Karate on the main islands, and in 1933 the Dai Nippon Butoku Kai recognized Karate as a Japanese martial way. After Funakoshi, having been inspired by the idea of "emptiness" in the Buddhist Heart Sūtra, changed the characters of Karate from "Tang Hand" to "Empty Hand," this became the most widely used spelling.   (Mark Winchester)

生活の中の伝統芸術と工芸

　日本の伝統文化と一言で言っても、そこには色々なものが含まれます。海外でよく知られている日本の文化と言えば華道、茶道を始め、能楽や歌舞伎、落語などの芸能、剣道・柔道などの武道、俳句や短歌などの文学がまず挙げられるでしょう。雅楽のように大陸を起源とするものもありますが、それらは日本の中で再編成され、独自の文化として発展を遂げてきました。

　生活の中で見られる伝統文化の1つとして工芸品があります。特に漆器は日本を代表するものとして有名で、陶器を意味するchinaと同じく、海外ではjapanという別名がつけられています。フランス最後の王妃マリー・アントワネットやその母マリア・テレジアも漆器の愛好家として知られています。

　また日本の和紙も、その美しさと丈夫さで高い評価を受けています。2014年には「和紙〜日本の手漉和紙技術〜」がユネスコの無形文化遺産に登録されました。和紙の原料には色々ありますが、ここで登録対象になったのは和紙の材料に楮だけを使い、伝統的な技法をもって作られる細川紙（埼玉県）、本美濃紙（岐阜県）、石州半紙（島根県）の3紙のみです。

　日本らしさを表現するのに使われる言葉「和」。和紙の他、和食、和服、和室などにもその例を見ることができますが、厚い畳が一面に敷き詰められた和室が誕生したのは、中世以降のことです。それまでの畳は座る際の敷物や寝台代わりに一部使われているのみでした。

　伝統文化は古くから受け継がれてきたものですが、時代に合わせて多少形を変えていく場合があります。歌舞伎や能楽もアニメやボーカロイドの初音ミクを取り入れ、大衆文化とコラボした作品を作って若い世代に親しんでもらおうとしています。

（亀井ダイチ・アンドリュー）

Traditional Arts and Crafts in Japanese Life

Traditional Japanese culture incorporates many diverse art forms. Many are well-known overseas: one can readily think of examples starting with Ikebana and tea ceremony, performing arts such as Nō or Kabuki, martial arts such as Judō or Kendō, or literary forms such as Tanka and Haiku. Some originated from the continent, such as Gagaku, but were adapted and developed to become distinct parts of Japanese culture.

One form of traditional culture that can be seen in daily life is crafts (*kōgei*). Lacquerware (*shikki*) is particularly famous for representing Japan overseas, and came to be called "japan" much as porcelain came to be called "china." The last queen of France, Marie Antoinette, and her mother, Empress Maria Theresa, were well-known as aficionados of lacquerware.

Another craft is Japanese paper (*washi*), which has been highly valued for its beauty and durability. In 2014, "*Washi*, craftsmanship of traditional Japanese hand-made paper" was inscribed as an Intangible Cultural Heritage by UNESCO. Many materials can be used to produce *washi*, but only the traditional techniques that employ fibers from paper mulberry plants to produce three types of *washi* — Hosokawa-shi (Saitama Prefecture), Hon-minoshi (Gifu Prefecture), and Sekishū-banshi (Shimane Prefecture) — were inscribed.

Japanese styles are identified with the prefix "*wa-*." Aside from *washi*, examples include *washoku* (Japanese cuisine), *wafuku* (Japanese clothing), and *washitsu* (Japanese room). *Washitsu* brings to mind a room with thick *tatami* (rice straw) mats covering the floor, but this only dates from the middle ages. Until then, *tatami* mats had been just partially used as cushions or beds.

While traditional culture is something that has been passed down from long ago, there are cases where it changes form according to the times. For example, there have been Kabuki and Nō performances inspired by anime or the vocaloid Hatsune Miku. Such works, produced through collaboration with pop culture, seek to appeal to the younger generation.

(A. T. Kamei-Dyche)

❖日本の世界文化遺産❖

❸ 古都京都の文化財
Historic Monuments of Ancient Kyoto

《平安から江戸までの歴史と文化を伝える千年の都》

　794年の平安京建都から明治維新後に東京に首都が移転されるまで、京都は日本の都として貴族、武士、王朝が築いた時代の舞台となったところです。古都京都には、それぞれの時代の文化を示す文化財が数多く残されています。1000年を超える歴史を映し出す2000件を超える文化財を代表して、16社寺と1城が世界文化遺産に登録されました。

【所在地】京都府・滋賀県　【登録年】1994年
【写　真】天龍寺（提供：天龍寺）

4
自然との共生
Coexisting with Nature

4｜自然との共生

《関東大震災》
炎上する帝国劇場（左）と警視庁（右）
（東京都復興記念館所蔵資料）

《関東大震災》
復興事業で建設され今も使用されている清洲橋（東京・中央区／江東区）

《阪神・淡路大震災》
倒壊した高速道路
（写真提供：神戸市）

【関東大震災】

　1923年9月1日正午少し前、関東地方南部を震源とするマグニチュード7.9の地震が発生しました。発生時刻が昼時で、調理のために火を使用していた場所が多かったため、同時多発的に火災が発生しました。火事は強風によって燃え広がって大火災となり、東京、横浜などが壊滅的な被害を受けました。死者・行方不明者は約10万5千人に上り、日本史上最大の被害を出した自然災害です。

　中央政府も被災し、新聞などの情報伝達手段も失われたため、被災地周辺では、不安に陥った人々の間に流言が飛び交いました。そのため、「震災に乗じて朝鮮人（当時朝鮮は日本の植民地統治下にありました）や社会主義者が放火や暴行を行っている」という虚偽のうわさを信じた日本人によって、朝鮮人や中国人、社会主義者が殺傷される事件も発生しました。

　震災からの復興の過程で、街路や建物が整備され、東京は近代的な都市に生まれ変わりました。

【阪神・淡路大震災】

　1995年1月17日午前6時前、兵庫県南部を震源とするマグニチュード7.3の地震が発生しました。野島断層の活動による直下型地震でした。発生時刻が早朝であったため、まだ眠っている間に激しい揺れに襲われ、倒壊した家屋や家具の下敷きとなり亡くなった人が多く出ました。大規模な火災も発生しました。この地震により、神戸市を中心に約6400人の死者・行方不明者が出ました。

The Great Kantō Earthquake

On September 1, 1923, shortly before noon, there occurred a 7.9 magnitude earthquake with the epicenter in the southern part of the Kantō area. It struck at lunchtime, when many people were cooking meals, and as a result many fires broke out at the same time. Because of the strong wind, the small isolated fires merged, and Tokyo, Yokohama, and other areas were completely devastated. The number of casualties, including deaths and people who went missing, rose to about 105,000, making it the biggest natural disaster to ever hit Japan.

The central government was also affected, and newspapers and other means of conveying information were not functional, so various rumors started spreading among the people in the stricken areas. There were also incidents of Japanese people who believed false reports that "Koreans (at the time, the Korean Peninsula was a Japanese colony) and socialists are taking advantage of the earthquake and committing arson and violence," and beat or killed Koreans, Chinese, and socialists.

In the reconstruction process following the disaster, new roads and buildings were erected, and Tokyo was reborn as a modern city.

The Great Hanshin Earthquake

On January 17, 1995, just before 6 a.m., a 7.3 magnitude earthquake struck, with the epicenter in the southern part of Hyōgo Prefecture. It occurred directly underneath the region, along the Nojima fault. Since it was early in the morning and many people were still sleeping, there were a lot of victims who died caught under the debris from the houses or under the furniture. A large-scale fire also broke out. There were about 6,400 casualties, including deaths and people missing, especially in the city of Kōbe.

Besides the large number of victims, the bullet train tracks

《阪神・淡路大震災》
大規模な火災
（写真提供：神戸市）

多数の死者を出したこと、耐震性を考慮してつくられていたはずの新幹線の線路や高速道路も倒壊したことなどから、日本人は改めて地震の恐ろしさを知ることになりました。

この震災をきっかけに日本社会でボランティア活動がさかんになりました。また、グローバル化を反映し、海外からも救援隊が訪れるなどの温かい支援がありました。

【東日本大震災】

2011年3月11日午後3時前、東北地方太平洋沖を震源とするマグニチュード9.0の地震が発生しました。日本は地震が多い国ですが、この地震は観測史上最大の超巨大地震でした。

巨大津波が東北から関東の太平洋岸を襲い、多くの人々の命を奪いました。宮城や岩手、福島を中心に死者・行方不明者は約2万人に上りました。東京電力福島第一原子力発電所では、津波の被害により原子炉を冷却できなくなり、大量の放射性物質を放出する深刻な事故が発生しました。

突然発生した、広範囲に及ぶ災害に際して、人々は互いに助け合い、秩序正しく行動しました。被災地を支援する動きは日本全国に広がり、たくさんのボランティアが被災地に向かいました。

《東日本大震災》
押し寄せる津波（仙台市）
（写真提供：仙台市）

いっそうのグローバル化とインターネットの発達などを反映し、世界各地から救援隊が訪れたり、義援金や励ましのメッセージが寄せられたりしました。

いまも被災地では復興と、事故を起こした福島原発の廃炉のための作業が続けられています。

（土田宏成）

《東日本大震災》
陸に打ち上げられた漁船（写真出所：東日本大震災文庫（宮城県）／提供：気仙沼土木事務所）

and the suspended highways, which were supposed to have been designed to withstand such a temblor, also crashed down. This reminded Japanese people just how powerful such an earthquake could be.

This disaster marked the spreading of volunteer activities within Japanese society. As a sign of globalization, there was also a lot of international support, including rescue teams that came from abroad.

The Great East Japan Earthquake

On March 11, 2011, before 3 p.m., there occurred a magnitude 9.0 earthquake with the epicenter off the Pacific coast of the Tōhoku region. For earthquake-prone Japan, this was the biggest megathrust earthquake to have ever been recorded in history.

A giant tsunami wave hit the east coast from Tōhoku to Kantō, taking the lives of many victims. The number of casualties rose to about 20,000, particularly in Miyagi, Iwate, and Fukushima Prefectures. At the Fukushima Dai-ichi Nuclear Power Station operated by TEPCO, the tsunami disabled the reactor cooling systems and large quantities of radioactive substances was released into the atmosphere, making it a very serious accident.

Faced with this large-scale disaster that hit unexpectedly, people reacted in an orderly fashion, helping each other. Initiatives to support the affected regions spread throughout Japan, and many people headed to the stricken areas as volunteers.

As a sign of the increasing globalization and of the spread of the internet, rescue teams came from abroad, and a lot of donations and support messages were sent from all over the world.

Reconstruction work in the affected areas and cleaning operations at the Fukushima Dai-ichi Nuclear Power Station are still under way.   (Tr. R. Paşca)

【農業】

　お米は日本文化において単なる食糧品ではなく、非常に長い歴史を有する霊的な存在のようなものです。土器に残っている炭化した籾や米の跡、そして各地に確認された水田用の溝の跡から、日本では稲作が縄文時代中期に行われ始めたことが分かります。日本人にとって祖先の時代から重要かつ身近な存在だったということです。

　現在でも日本中で行われている多くの神事やお祭りでは、お米はお酒や塩などとならび神様に供物として奉納されるものの1つです。日本人の米に対する思い入れは非常に強く、極めて大切な食べ物とされてきました。お米は農業の産物ではなく、ヒトとカミとの関係をも表す穀物であるからです。

　さらに、長期保存できることからお米には経済的価値もあります。例えば、江戸時代には年貢として使われたり、「石高」を基に身分秩序の基準として用いられたりなどして、日本の社会に様々な形で浸透してきていると言えます。

田に実る稲穂

【共生】

　地震や風水害などによる災害が非常に多い日本ですが、この国土に住む人々にとっては自然の無常は昔から伝わってきた記憶であり、身体に染み付いている遺伝子のようなものだと言えます。そして、その記憶こそが日本人の自然観の根底にあるに違いありません。

　古代の日本人は、「自然」を人間に対する1つの総体的なものではなく、世の中の物すべてが個別的で

Agriculture

In Japanese culture, rice is more than just simple food: it is a sort of spiritual presence that has a very long history. From the carbonized traces of husks and grains left inside earthen pots, and from the remains of ditches for rice paddies discovered throughout the country, we know that rice cultivation began in Japan somewhere around the mid-Jōmon period. In other words, rice has been for Japanese people a very important and familiar presence since the times of their ancestors.

Even today, rice is one of the offerings presented to gods in various religious rituals and festivals all across Japan, along with sake and salt. The feelings Japanese people have toward rice are very intense, and it has been considered as one of the essential foods. Rice is not just a simple product of agriculture, it is a cereal that also expresses the connection between human beings and gods.

Moreover, rice also has an economic value because it can be preserved over long periods of time. For example, during the Edo period it was used to pay the annual tribute, or as a basis for determining one's social status depending on the amount of rice harvested on the domain (*kokudaka*). Rice has permeated Japanese society in a variety of ways.

Symbiosis

Japan is a country of many disasters caused by earthquakes, wind, or water, and for the people living on this land the impermanence of Nature is both a memory passed down through generations, and something akin to a genetic inheritance embedded within their bodies. And it is this very memory that lies at the foundation of Japanese people's view of Nature.

In ancient times, the Japanese did not see Nature as a generic unitary entity in opposition with humanity. Instead, they tended to interpret the world around them as a collection of a myriad separate, individual things. This way of thinking sees gods,

あり、その無数の個体の集合として捉える傾向が強かったようです。そのような思想のもと、カミ・ヒト・自然の三者は区別のつかない存在として、密接に結ばれているという関係にあります。

言い換えてみると、つまり人間は自然と対峙(たいじ)するものではなく、自然の中に含まれてその一部として共存している、という考え方です。このエコロジカルな視点には、アニミズム的発想や仏教的思想の要素も含まれていますが、これは日本人の自然観の大きな特徴の1つと言えるでしょう。

【安藤昌益(しょうえき)(1703-1762)】

明治維新まで「自然」は「山川草木」、「花鳥風月」、「山河大地」などと呼ばれていました。「自然」とは「自らなる」という意味で、形容詞または副詞として使われていました。

しかし、江戸時代に『自然真営道』というタイトルで「自然」について語った人物がいます。それが、身分制度や幕藩体制などの社会を「法の世」と称して批判し、「自然の世」という理想の世界像を描き、それを「直耕(ちょっこう)」や「転定(てんち)」など、独自の言葉で表した独創的な思想家、安藤昌益です。昌益は社会の矛盾を目の当たりにし、貧富の差も支配階級もない平等な世の中を掲げ、オリジナルの思想を生み出しました。

昌益にとって、「自然」とは世界全体そのものであり、人間はその中の必要不可欠な1つの構成要素です。つまり、人間が自然の中で自然と共に生きるというのが唯一の「真」の道であるという考え方です。

(ロマン・パシュカ)

『稿本 自然真営道』
(東京大学総合図書館所蔵資料)

八戸市安藤昌益資料館
(写真提供：安藤昌益資料館を育てる会)

human beings, and Nature as three inseparable entities among which there is a deep connection.

In other words, human beings must not exploit Nature, but should instead coexist as part of it, in harmony. This ecological worldview incorporates animistic and Buddhist elements, and it is one of the most important characteristics of the Japanese view of Nature.

Andō Shōeki

Until the Meiji Restoration, Japanese people would refer to "Nature" by using compounds such as *sansensōmoku* ("mountains, rivers, grass, tree"), *kachōfūgetsu* ("flowers, birds, wind, moon"), or *sangadaichi* ("mountains, rivers, earth"). The word *shizen* was used rather as an adjective or an adverb, and its meaning was "spontaneous creation."

However, in the Edo period there was a philosopher who talked about "Nature" (*shizen*) in several writings gathered under the title *The True Way of Nature*. His name was Andō Shōeki (1703-1762). He was a unique thinker who criticized society, particularly the class system and the Tokugawa shogunate, by calling it the "world of the law" (*hō no yo*), and proposed instead a vision of the world as the "world of nature" (*shizen no yo*) which he described by using original concepts like "direct cultivation" (*chokkō*), or "dynamic heaven-and-earth" (*tenchi*). Shōeki was a direct witness to various social contradictions and injustices, and he created a very original system of thought whereby he put forth a vision of the world in which everybody is equal, without any disparity in wealth and without any ruling class.

For Shōeki, "Nature" (*shizen*) was the world itself in its entirety, and human beings were an indispensable element within it. In other words, for him the only "true" way was for individuals to live as part of Nature and in communion with it.

(R. Paşca)

自然と災害

　日本は、世界で最も産業化が進んだ国の1つですが、自然が豊かな国でもあります。日本の国土は、北海道・本州・四国・九州・沖縄本島をはじめとする約7000の島々によって形成されています。その約3/4は山地で、山地の大部分は森林に覆われています。

　一方で日本は自然災害の多い国でもあります。日本周辺には4枚のプレートが存在し、海のプレートが陸のプレートの下に沈み込み、互いに影響し合って複雑な動きをしています。そのため、地殻変動が激しく、起伏に富んだ国土が形成されました。地震が多いのも、火山活動が活発なのも、同じ理由からです。

　国土の多くが温暖湿潤気候に属し、雨や雪が多く降ります。夏から秋にかけては台風が襲来します。

　海、山、豊富な雨、そしてそこに暮らす人々によって、日本の風景がつくられてきました。自然が豊かであることと災害が多いことは、表裏一体の関係なのです。

　火山活動に基づく地形や温泉は、観光資源であるばかりではありません。富士山のように芸術作品に描かれたり、その高さや噴火の恐ろしさから信仰の対象とされたり、日本人の文化や精神性にも影響を与えています。

　農業、漁業を通じて恵みをもたらしてくれる大地や海・川も、時々地震や津波、洪水などによって、人々に災いをもたらしてきました。日本の国土は山が多いため、平らで広い土地を得やすい川の下流や海沿いに広がる平野に人口が集中することになりました。その傾向は、近代になって都市化が進むにつれいっそう強まりました。平野は土地が低く地盤も不安定なため、水害や津波の被害を受けやすく、地震の揺れも大きくなります。

　自然の恵みを生かしつつ、災害にどのように対処するか。これが今も昔も日本列島に住む人々の課題なのです。　　　（土田宏成）

Nature and Disasters

Japan is one of the most industrialized nations in the world, and it is also a country with a rich and beautiful nature. Japan's territory comprises about 7,000 islands, including Hokkaidō, Honshū, Shikoku, Kyūshū and Okinawa Main Island. About three quarters of the land is mountainous, and the mountains are heavily forested.

But Japan is also a country of many natural disasters. There are four plates around Japan, and they influence each other in complex movements, with the sea plates sinking under the continental ones. The earth's crust is extremely unstable and this led to the formation of a land with many irregularities and bumps. This is why there are so many earthquakes and so many active volcanoes.

Most of the territory belongs to the humid subtropical climate, with a lot of rainfall and snowfall. From summer to autumn, several typhoons hit the country.

The Japanese landscape was shaped by the sea, the mountains, the heavy rainfall, and by the people living here. The beautiful nature and the numerous disasters are just two sides of the same coin.

The sharp relief and the hotsprings produced by the volcanic activity are more than just a tourist attraction. Mount Fuji, for example, has been depicted in many artistic works, while its height and the majesty of its eruptions have turned it into an object of religious beliefs that have had a great influence on the culture and spirituality of the Japanese people.

The land, the sea, and the rivers have offered many blessings through agriculture or fishing, but they have also caused a lot of damage through earthquakes, tsunami, or floods. Since the territory is mountainous, people settled in the plains in the lower reaches of rivers or by the ocean, where it is easier to find flat stretches of land. This tendency became stronger with the spread of urbanization in the modern period. In the plains, however, the ground is very low and unstable, and therefore prone to disasters such as tsunami or floods. The tremor of earthquakes is also bigger.

How do we cope with disasters and at the same time enjoy Nature's gifts? This has been and will remain one of the biggest problems for the people living in the Japanese archipelago.

(Tr. R. Paşca)

❖日本の世界文化遺産❖

白川郷・五箇山の合掌造り集落
Historic Villages of Shirakawa-go and Gokayama

《厳しい自然環境に育まれた独自の文化》

　岐阜県の白川村、富山県の平村、上平村の３つの集落が世界文化遺産に登録されています。「合掌造り」と呼ばれる独特の家の造りは、豪雪地域という厳しい自然環境とこの地の伝統的な生活文化によって生まれました。現在も、この周囲の自然環境の調和した遺産の中で人が生活し、独特の風景を私たちに見せてくれます。

【所在地】岐阜県・富山県　【登録年】1995年
【写　真】冬の合掌造り（提供：岐阜県白川村役場）

5
日本人の心
A Japanese Sense of Self

【朱子学】

　朱子学は、宋の朱熹が生み出した儒学の新しい学派です。朱熹は、原理ないし法則的なものである「理」が、世界、人間を貫く普遍的なものとして存在すると考えました。「理」に従って行為することが正しいと考えたため、政治については体制の維持、人間については自分の心の反省が重視されました。朱子学は、その後、儒学の正統という地位を獲得しました。

　日本では、江戸時代になると、朱子学は武士の思想として受け入れられました。朱子学は、社会的には武士の支配制度を「理」に即したものであると説明しました。また、道徳的には、「理」に従って欲望を抑える禁欲主義が重視されました。

　ところが、日本では、「理」を強調し、感情や欲望を否定する朱子学の思想は、全面的には受け入れられませんでした。そこで、朱子学に批判的な思想が相次いで出現したのです。（⇨66頁「儒教」）

【国学】

本居宣長
（写真提供：本居宣長記念館）

　国学は、日本文化の伝統を日本人の立場から研究する学問です。日本では、学問や文学は、長い間、漢文を使うものでした。しかし、日本には、日本語の伝統的な文体である和文が存在し、それを用いた和歌や物語が書かれました。本居宣長は、こうした文学の代表作である『源氏物語』の研究に取り組みました。そして、人間にとってもっとも重要なことは、「もののあはれ」すなわち感情、感動を持つこと、および、表現を通して、それに共感することであると説きました。彼は、これこそが日本の本来の文化伝統

Neo-Confucianism

Neo-Confucianism was a new branch of Confucianism developed by Zhu Xi during the Song dynasty. Zhu Xi maintained that *li* ("the principle") is a universal existence that underlies everything, from humanity to the world itself. He believed that individuals should act in accordance with the principle, and so he placed great importance on the preservation of the political system and on moral reflection. Later on, Neo-Confucianism gained recognition as a legitimate school.

In Edo-period Japan, Neo-Confucianism was associated with the way of thinking of the *bushi* warriors. Neo-Confucianism explained the warriors' social status as a ruling class as being in accordance with the principle *li*. From an ethical point of view, a lot of importance was also placed on frugality, the repression of desires in accordance with the principle.

However, Neo-Confucian thought, which emphasized the principle and denied sentiments and desires, was not adopted in its entirety. On the contrary, there emerged many schools of thought that were critical toward Neo-Confucianism (see the entry on Confucianism, p. 67).

Kokugaku ("National Study")

Kokugaku ("National Study") was an academic movement that promoted the study of the tradition of Japanese culture from the perspective of the Japanese. In Japan, in scholarship as well as in literature, Chinese writing was used for a long time. However, the traditional style of writing in Japanese, the so-called *wabun*, also existed in parallel, and many poems and stories were written in *wabun*. Motoori Norinaga began to study *Genji monogatari*, one of the most representative works of traditional literature. He proposed that the most important thing for human beings is to have *mono no aware* ("the pathos of things"), i. e. to have feelings and emotions and, by expressing them, to elicit and inspire empathy. For him, this was the true tradition of Japanese culture, and he called this way of thinking *yamato gokoro* ("the Japanese spirit"). He emphasized the idea that ethics and politics

であると考え、そのような精神を「大和心(やまとごころ)」と呼びました。道徳や政治は「もののあはれ」を抑圧するもので、否定すべきだと主張しました。宣長は、抑圧的な傾向は、知性を重視する中国の文化の影響によるものだと考えました。その後、『古事記』を研究して、『古事記伝』を書きました。彼は、日本の文化の本質を解明しようとしたのです。

平田篤胤(あつたね)は、宣長の影響を受け、日本文化の中に魂の行方を教える宗教的な内容を求めました。篤胤の影響を受けた国学者たちは、日本文化の優越性を主張し、外国の文化を拒否しようとしたため、明治になると、近代化に対応することができなくなってしまいます。しかし、国学の持つ合理的な研究としての側面は、西洋の学問の影響を受けつつ、日本に関するさまざまな分野の研究に受け継がれました。

平田篤胤
(立野家所蔵:千葉県文書館提供)

【水戸学】

水戸学は、幕末の水戸藩で当時の社会状況を背景として成立した思想です。代表的な思想家に藤田幽谷(ゆうこく)、会沢正志斎(せいしさい)がいます。

彼らはロシアの来航などによって生じた危機意識を背景に、国家のあり方を追求しました。会沢正志斎は、日本の国家のあり方を国体という概念に求め、天皇を中心とする国家像を打ち出しました。また、外国に対してはそれを日本から排除する攘夷を説きました。彼の思想は、幕末の尊王攘夷の運動の理論として大きな影響を与えたのです。

明治になると、その極端な排外主義的な主張は、国家主義的な思想に影響を与え、日本の社会の反近代主義的な傾向の根拠となりました。　　（窪田高明）

会沢正志斎
(個人蔵)

should be rejected because they suppressed *mono no aware*. His interpretation was that the cause of this tendency to suppress resides in the influence of Chinese culture, which favors the intellect. Later on, he studied *Kojiki* ("Records of Ancient Matters") and wrote *Kojikiden* ("Commentary on the *Kojiki*"). He tried to clarify the true essence of Japanese culture.

Hirata Atsutane, influenced by Norinaga, searched for a religious element that would indicate the presence of a spirit, or "soul" (*tamashii*), within Japanese culture. *Kokugaku* scholars who were influenced by Atsutane emphasized the superiority of Japanese culture and tried to reject foreign cultures, and therefore they could not adapt to modernization during the Meiji period. However, *Kokugaku*'s inclination for rational study, while influenced by Western disciplines, was inherited in various research fields related to Japan.

The Mito School

The Mito School was a movement that appeared against the social background of the final years of the Edo period in the Mito province. Among the most representative thinkers are Fujita Yūkoku and Aizawa Seishisai.

With a sense of impending crisis caused, among other things, by the arrival of Russian ships, they started to reflect on what a state should be. Aizawa Seishisai theorized the existence and meaning of the state using the concept of *kokutai* ("national polity"), and put forth an image of the state with the Emperor at its center. He also advocated the exclusion of foreigners from Japan. His philosophy exerted a big influence on the *sonnō jōi* movement ("revere the emperor, expel the barbarians") at the end of the Edo period.

In the Meiji period, these extreme chauvinistic views influenced notions of the state and became the basis for anti-modernist tendencies in Japanese society. (Tr. R. Paşca)

【自分】

「自分」という感覚は、多様な人間関係から構築される自己意識です。その認識には、家族や学校など社会全体の人々からの眼差しが反映されています。

人と人との間でその都度形成される状況が「空気」で、期待に応えて行動をとることが「空気を読む」ことです。自分は、周囲の様子から、何が期待されているのかを感じます。相手が望むことや多様な状況に配慮し適切な行動をとることが求められます。あえて逸脱して「空気を読まない」人を「KY」と言います。

「空気」が社会で固定化されると「世間」になります。自分の行動を評価する観客が「世間」です。世間には、社会全体の人たちが重んじる価値や規範があります。自分という感覚に、この世間の評価が入り、多様な状況に応えようとします。自分とは、外部からの影響に左右されない独立した個人ではなく、多様な人たちの期待や美意識に応じていく流動的存在です。

【精神】

精神は自分の内面を鍛練していき、簡単には屈することのない強い意志を生みます。心を磨き、心の調和を得、健全な魂を育む(はぐく)ための原動力です。

高い精神性を日常の場面で表わすことが期待されています。学校、会社、家庭などでの日常生活の行動において、精神を高めるということが意識されます。勉強や社会の役割など、どのようなものでも、頑張り粘り強く対処していこうとすることが美徳とされます。学問に励むということや、仕事に集中するということ

Self

The sense of "self" is the personal awareness constructed through interactions with various individuals. This awareness is also a reflection of different perspectives from society at large, including members of the family or friends from school.

The context created by each and every human interaction is called *kūki* in Japanese ("air", or "atmosphere"), while acting according to the expectations of the other in such a context is to "read the air" (*kūki o yomu*). From the conditions of the surroundings, the self senses what is expected. The individual is supposed to act in accordance with the expectations of the interlocutor and with a variety of situations and conditions. People who ignore this deliberately are called "KY", as they cannot "read the air" (*kūki o yomanai*).

When the "air" is established within society, it becomes the "common public worldview" (*seken*), and it is the "public" that evaluates and judges the behavior of the self. The common worldview comprises the values and norms that are considered important by most people in society. The sense of self, under the effect of public evaluation, tries to adapt to various situations. The self is therefore not an independent entity free from external influences, but a fluid existence that constantly responds to the expectations and aesthetic principles of various people.

Spirit

Spirit shapes the inner self, thus forging a strong will that is not easily broken. Spirit is the dynamic force that refines the heart, gives peace of mind, and builds a healthy soul.

We are expected to display a high level of spirituality in many daily life situations. We are constantly trying to elevate our spirit through our behavior in daily life at school, in the workplace, or at home. Whether it is study or our social role, trying to do our best and be tenacious in all situations is seen as a virtue. Taking a challenge and learning something new, or concentrating on our work are methods through which we can elevate our spirit. Our effort to deal with the problems and difficulties we encounter is highly regarded.

剣道の稽古

も、精神を高める手段になります。そこでの課題や問題に懸命に勤しむ姿勢が高く評価されます。

毎日が、仲間と共に内面の精神を高め合い競い合う舞台になります。そこでは、例えば剣道など武道の稽古の場のように、勝ち負けを意識するというよりは、お互いに内面を磨き合うという関係を重んじます。

【母性】

日本社会は「母性社会」と言われています。日本人は、人間関係で情緒的な繋がりを重んじながら信頼関係を築いています。言葉を介さなくても、場の雰囲気で分かり合える関係を重んじるのが日本人のコミュニケーションの特徴です。

家で幼児が母親に依存するような関係から生まれてくる感覚です。この母性は、家庭外での多様な社会集団の成員にも見られます。家庭での母親の存在が象徴しているように、対人関係で、お互いを思い遣り認め合おうとする安堵感のある関係を重んじます。

母性は、日本人が対人関係で大切にする「甘え」の関係と結びついています。この概念は、相手の厚意を受動的に期待しながら、自分が相手と互いに依存し合う関係を形成します。この母性的な意思疎通は、相手の状況や思いを察していくものです。社会の様々な場で、相手を気遣い配慮しながら、相互理解する関係を形成します。　　　　（吉田光宏）

母と子

Each and every day gives us the opportunity to compete with our peers to elevate our spirit. Like in martial arts practice, for example in *kendō*, the important thing is not who wins or loses, but to establish an interaction in which we mutually refine our inner spirit.

Maternity

Japanese society is often called a "matriarchal society." Japanese people build trust relationships among themselves by placing importance on emotional connections. One of the characteristics of the communication style of Japanese people is to emphasize relationships where one understands their interlocutor based solely on the atmosphere of the environment, without using any words.

This communication style stems from the relationship of dependence created at home between mother and child. The reliance on a mother figure is also seen in members of various social groups outside the home. As symbolized by the presence of the mother in the family, this is a relationship of compassion and acceptance of the other where one feels safe and relieved.

The idea of maternity is linked to the *amae* ("dependence") that Japanese people attach great value to in interpersonal relationships. This concept refers to building a relationship where, while passively expecting kindness from the interlocutor, one becomes mutually dependent with that interlocutor. The key in this maternal connection is to grasp the interlocutor's circumstances and thoughts. Showing concern and consideration toward the other in various social situations forges a relationship of mutual understanding. (Tr. R. Paşca)

現代社会で働く独身女性の世界観

　男女格差を調査した2017年の国際比較では、日本は144か国中114位です。男女雇用機会均等法が制定されて約30年経ても、男性と同等に働く女性は少数です。職場の正規雇用社員は、男性が8割なのに対し、女性は4割です。女性の場合、男性と平等な形で働く「総合職」と、その仕事の補佐的役割をする「一般職」に分けられます。男性の8割が総合職ですが、女性の総合職は1割で、9割が男性社員の補佐をする一般職です。女性一般職の約半数が非正規雇用者です。男性の平均給与水準を100とすれば、女性はおよそ70に留まります。このように日本の男性中心社会の現状が数字に表われています。

　日本の会社内で、女性は「長時間労働や深夜労働をさせづらい」とみられがちで、結婚後は「家事責任や育児休暇も考慮する必要がある」とみられがちです。一方、20代の働く独身女性たちは男性同等の仕事は「きつい」と考え「年収300万円で、仕事は必要なだけこなし、プライベートを楽しむ」スタイルを支持する傾向があります。日本では「母業」に美徳があり、「主婦業」が社会で大切な役割として位置づけられています。女性たちの多くは「そこそこの幸せ」で「専業主婦」願望をもち、好きなことを「趣味的仕事」として持つ「新専業主婦志向」を支持します。女性たちは、今後会社で活躍することがこれまで以上に求められています。現状では、あえて昇進は望まず、男性同様の苦労はしたくないという女性が8割を占めます。女性の「専業主婦志向」の背景には、日本の会社の男性中心的制度があります。また、家族は夫と共に子に愛情を注げる「かけがえのない関係」を形成できる居場所だという規範もあります。

（吉田光宏）

The Worldview of Working Single Women

In a 2017 survey on gender gap, Japan ranked 114th out of 144 countries. Thirty years after the adoption of the Equal Employment Act, there are still few women who work in the same conditions as men. The proportion of regular employees on permanent contracts is 80% for men, but only 40% for women. For women, there are two main categories of jobs: "regular jobs," where they have the same positions as men, and "administrative jobs," with an auxiliary role. 80% of the men have "regular jobs" with prospects for promotion, whereas only 10% of women have regular jobs and 90% of them have administrative jobs. About half of the women employed in administrative jobs have non-permanent contracts. If we consider the standard pay for men as 100, then for women it remains around 70. As can be seen from these figures, Japanese society is a male-centered one.

In Japanese companies, there is a strong tendency to think that "it's difficult to have women work overtime," and that "after marriage women have the responsibility of house chores, and they need maternal leave." On the other hand, among single working women in their 20s there is a tendency to consider a job equal to that of a man as being "tough," and to adopt a lifestyle of "working for an annual income of about 3,000,000 yen, just enough to enjoy a full personal life." In Japan, accomplishing one's duty as a mother is seen as a virtue, and being a housewife is considered a very important role in society. Many women actually endorse this "new housewife mentality" by pursuing a career as housewives, with "a little bit of happiness" and "a job more like a hobby" where they can do what they want. Expectations are higher than before for women to be more active in companies from now on. At present, 80% of women have no desire to be promoted as they do not want to go through the same hardships as men. Behind the "housewife mentality" lies the reality of the male-centered Japanese social system. There is also the perception that the home is the place where women can form a "unique bond" with their family by bestowing love on their husband and children.

(Tr. R. Paşca)

❖日本の世界文化遺産❖

広島平和記念碑(原爆ドーム)
Hiroshima Peace Memorial (Genbaku Dome)

《人類共通の平和記念碑》

　他の登録地が人類の長い歴史や文化を伝えるのに対し、この原爆ドームは、1945年に人類史上初めて使用された核兵器の傷あとを伝える建造物です。時代を超えて、核兵器が世界からなくなることや平和の大切さを訴えつづける人類共通の記念碑といえます。世界には、他にもこのような平和を呼びかける世界遺産がいくつかあります。

【所在地】広島県　【登録年】1996年
【写　真】原爆ドーム(提供:広島県)

6 宗教と日本人

Religion and the Japanese People

【神道】

　神道とは、日本で生まれたさまざまな神を信じる信仰をひろく指す言葉です。神道といっても、共通する教典や教義をもつ１つの宗教が存在するわけではありません。神への信仰は、特定の地域、集団に結びついて成立しています。神とそれを信じる人々、神を祀る儀式が神道の中心です。それぞれの神や神社は、その成立を述べた縁起という物語を持っています。日本各地には多くの神が共存し、それを信じる人々によって支えられてきました。

　日本の神にはいくつかのタイプが存在します。１つは祖先の神です。もう１つは、私たちの外の世界からやってくる神です。また、御霊といって、人々に大きな災厄を与えるタイプもあります。この神は祀られることによって、人々を守り、利益を与える存在に変化します。

　中世になると、神道も教義や教団を作るようになりますが、仏教のように大規模な教団は生まれませんでした。明治になると、天皇を中心とする国家観にそって、天照大神を中心とする国家神道が作られましたが、敗戦とともに解体されました。

天照大神を祀る伊勢神宮（Ⓒ伊勢志摩観光コンベンション機構）

【仏教】

　仏教は、インドの釈迦が始めた宗教です。釈迦は、心の執着を捨てて、真実に目覚めることを説きました。しかし、それが中国や朝鮮を経て、日本に伝わると、悟りの宗教としてではなく、祈禱によって魔術的な力を発揮する宗教として受け入れられました。朝廷はその魔術的な力を独占し、みずからの支配体制を守る

Shinto

Shinto broadly refers to a faith in spirits or phenomena known as *kami* that have their origins in Japan. Despite referring to this faith as Shinto, it does not consist of a single religion with a set scripture or doctrine. Faith in the *kami* is established through the *kami's* ties with specific regions and groups of people. The *kami* and those who believe in them, and the rituals for worshiping the *kami*, lie at the heart of Shinto. Each *kami* and Shinto shrine has an auspicious story regarding its origins. *Kami* co-exist in regions all over Japan and they are supported by the people that believe in them.

There are several different types of Japanese *kami*. One example would be the *kami* of one's ancestors. Another example would be *kami* who come from a different world to our own. There are also spirits of *kami*, known as *goryō*, that can cause huge natural disasters. Through worshiping *goryō* they change into *kami* that protect and benefit people.

In the medieval period, Shinto began to create a kind of religious doctrine and form sects. However, unlike Buddhism, large-scale religious sects did not appear. In the Meiji period, state Shinto was created in line with the national mood, which was centered on the Emperor. State Shinto had Amaterasu-ōmikami at the center of its belief system. However, with the Japanese defeat in the war, state Shinto ceased to exist.

Buddhism

Buddhism is a religion started by the Buddha in India. The Buddha preached that people should discard the obsessions of their minds and awaken themselves to the truth. However, when Buddhism was transmitted to Japan via China and Korea, instead of a religion of enlightenment, it was accepted as a religion that exerts a kind of mystical power through the act of prayer. The Imperial Court sought to monopolize this mystical power and use it to protect their regime. In the Heian period, an

ために利用しました。平安時代になると、呪術的な仏教である密教が広がりました。その一方で、阿弥陀仏による救済を説く浄土教が広く信じられるようになりました。(⇨68頁、70頁「仏」)

江戸時代になると、仏教は、政治権力によって管理されるようになり、自由な活動は制限されました。その活動は、葬儀などの死に係わる儀式が主なものとなりました。最近では、葬儀に僧侶を招かない形のものも増え、仏教の影響力は低下しています。

【儒教】

儒教は、孔子が中国の文化を背景にして作り上げた思想で、道徳、政治、宗教などを含んでいます。孔子の死後、中国の中心的な思想になりました。日本にも伝わりましたが、古代から中世にかけては、主として支配階級や知識人の教養にとどまり、日本人全体に影響を与えることはありませんでした。

江戸時代になると、武士を中心に朱子学(⇨52頁「朱子学」)が正統の学問として受け入れられるようになり、儒教は日本人にひろく影響するようになりました。ただし、日本の儒教の特徴は、朱子学に批判的な思想が大きな影響力を持ったことです。

中江藤樹、熊沢蕃山、伊藤仁斎、荻生徂徠などが儒教の代表的な研究者です。彼らに共通するのは、人間の感情や欲望を認める現実的な姿勢です。この傾向は、合理的な思考を育て、日本の近代化に貢献しました。近代になると、儒教は現実に対応できない思想と考えられるようになり、学ぶ人も減っていきました。

(窪田高明)

中江藤樹
(藤樹書院蔵)

esoteric form of Buddhism known as *mikkyō* spread widely throughout Japan. Meanwhile, Pure Land Buddhism, which preaches salvation through the Amida Buddha also came to be widely believed (see the entry on Mikkyō, Jōdokyō, and Zen, p.69, 71).

In the Edo period, Buddhism came under political control and its previous freedoms were curtailed. The main role of Buddhism in society became holding funerals and other rituals related to death. In recent years funerals to which Buddhist monks are not invited have increased and the influence of Buddhism is on the decline.

Confucianism

Confucianism is a system of ideas that Confucius (Kōshi, Kongzi) created within the context of Chinese culture and which includes aspects that are ethical, political and religious. After Confucius' death, Confucianism became a central system of thought in China. Confucianism was also introduced to Japan, but from the ancient to medieval periods its influence was limited to the education of the ruling classes and intellectuals, and it did not have a great influence on Japanese people as a whole.

In the Edo period, the Neo-Confucianism of Zhu Xi, known in Japanese as *Shushigaku* (see the entry on Neo-Confucianism, p.53) became accepted as a legitimate subject for study particularly among the *bushi* warrior classes. From then on, Confucianism began to widely influence Japanese people. A key feature of Confucianism in Japan is that ideas critical of *Shushigaku* came to exert a heavy influence on society.

Nakae Tōju, Kumazawa Banzan, Itō Jinsai and Ogyū Sorai are the representative scholars of this critical school. They all share the realistic attitude of recognizing people's feelings and desires. This trend fostered rational thought in Japan and contributed to Japan's modernization. In the modern era, however, Confucianism has come to be thought of as being unable to adapt to modern reality and thus the number of people learning about Confucianism has decreased. (Tr. M. Winchester)

【密教】

　密教（秘密の教え）は大乗仏教のなかの秘教です。インドでヒンドゥー教文化の影響のもと7世紀に成立した中期密教経典『大日経』『金剛頂経』によって体系化されました。

　平安時代前期（806年）に空海は唐から密教を伝えて真言宗を開き、従来の大乗仏教を顕教とよんで区別しました。空海以前に伝わっていた初期密教を雑密、空海の伝えた中期密教を純密といいます。最澄は天台宗を伝えましたが、円仁・円珍の代に密教化を強めました。密教は現世利益を得るための加持祈禱を行ったので、貴顕に歓迎されました。

　密教は修法のさいに曼荼羅などを本尊としたため密教美術が発達しました。密教はあまり中国化しないうちに日本まで伝わったので、インド風が認められます。インドやインドネシアに遺る中期密教の美術や後期密教を継承したチベット仏教とその美術から、かつての密教文化の広がりをうかがうことができます。

【浄土教】

　浄土教とは、仏菩薩の住む清浄な国土へ往生して悟りを得ようとする教えです。浄土三部経（『無量寿経』『阿弥陀経』『観無量寿経』）に説かれた阿弥陀仏の西方極楽浄土が信仰を集めました。

　日本では平安時代中期に天台宗で布教されるようになり、源信は『往生要集』（985年）を著して末法相応の教えとしての浄土教を説きました。天台浄土教は観想の修行を重視したため、観想の助けとなる浄土教美術が盛んになりました。末法到来の翌年（1053

Mikkyō

Mikkyō consists of secret, or esoteric, teachings of Mahāyāna Buddhism. It was systematized under the influence of Hindu culture in India through 7th-Century scriptures such as the Mahāvairocana Tantra and the Vajrasekhara Sutra.

During the early Heian period (806), Kūkai brought mikkyō teachings with him from Tang Dynasty China and founded Shingon Buddhism, distinguishing it from traditional Mahāyāna Buddhism, which came to be known as Kengyō. Early mikkyō teachings which reached Japan before Kūkai are known as *zōmitsu* (mixed), whereas the middle period mikkyō that Kūkai taught is known as *junmitsu* (pure). The monk Saichō is known for founding the Tendai sect, and under the guidance of Ennin and Enchin, the sect was esotericized. Mikkyō involved prayers made to obtain benefit in the present world and thus was welcomed by the aristocracy. Mikkyō art also developed, in particular through its use of mandala as a principle image.

Mikkyō entered Japan with little Sinicization and therefore is recognized for its Indian character. The spread of traditional mikkyō culture can be seen in the art of middle period mikkyō in India and Indonesia, as well as the late period mikkyō art of Tibetan Buddhism.

Jōdokyō

Jōdokyō, or Pure Land Buddhism, seeks enlightenment through passing to the celestial pure abode of Buddhas and the Bodhisattvas. The main articles of faith in Pure Land Buddhism are the Amitābha (Amida) Buddha and the Western Paradise as espoused in the Three Pure Land Sutras (the Infinite Life Sutra, the Amithaba Sutra, and the Amitayurdhyana Sutra).

In Japan during the mid-Heian period, Tendai sect Buddhism flourished and the Buddhist cleric Genshin, author of *Essentials of Birth in the Pure Land* (985), preached Pure Land Buddhism as a doctrine attune to a 'latter day' or 'age of decadence' (*mappō*) eschatology. Because Tendai Pure Land Buddhism places an emphasis on training in contemplation, Pure Land Buddhist art that aims to aid such training began to thrive. In the year following the introduction of *mappō* thought, the Byōdōin Temple was erected by Fujiwara Yorimichi in 1053 and reputed to have reproduced paradise on earth.

平等院鳳凰堂
（Ⓒ平等院）

年）に藤原頼通が造営した平等院鳳凰堂は、この世に極楽浄土を再現したと評されました。

鎌倉時代に入ると、法然が自らの思索を深めて『選択本願念仏集』（1198年）を著し、浄土宗を開きました。弟子の親鸞は浄土真宗を開きました。中世の長くつづいた戦乱の時代に、阿弥陀仏の本願力による救済を説いた浄土系宗派は幅広い階層に広まりました。現代でも諸宗派のなかで信者が多く、日本仏教の特色となっています。

【禅宗】

禅は精神統一を行うインドの伝統的修行法であるヨーガが仏教に取り入れられたもので、中国において坐禅を専らとする禅宗が成立しました。6世紀にインドから来た達磨を初祖としますが、中国で独自の発展を遂げました。

鎌倉時代に入宋した栄西は臨済宗を、道元は曹洞宗を伝えました。禅宗は武家の帰依を受けて日本に定着し、鎌倉五山・京都五山が定められて繁栄しました。日本からの招請もあって宋・元から多くの禅僧が渡来し、中国風の禅宗文化をもたらしました。のち1654年に来日した隠元は黄檗宗を開きました。

禅宗文化、例えば五山文学、禅宗様建築、作庭、墨跡、頂相（禅僧の肖像画）、水墨画、茶の湯、立花、能楽などは日本の中世文化の核となっており、禅宗を通して中国との文化交流を知ることができます。

禅の思想や文化は、鈴木大拙（1870-1966）の英語の著作や講演によって、海外でも広く知られるようになりました。
（吉村稔子）

In the Kamakura Period, the religious reformer, Hōnen, in an attempt to deepen his thinking wrote his *Senchaku Hongan Nembutsushū* (Passages on the Selection of the Nembutsu in the Original Vow, 1198) and founded the Jōdo-shū (Pure Land School). His disciple, Shinran, founded the Jōdo Shinshū (True Pure Land School). During the Middles Ages, in an era of long-lasting wars, Pure Land-based sects that preached salvation according to the present force of the Amitābha Buddha spread across a wide range of social classes in Japan. Even today, there are many followers of Pure Land Buddhism and it remains a characteristic feature of Japanese Buddhism.

Zen

Zen is a practice in which the traditional Indian training method of yoga — aimed at attaining spiritual unification — was incorporated into Buddhism and the Zen sect was established in China as a form of Buddhism specializing in the practice of *Zazen* (meditation). Its founder is said to be Bodhidharma who travelled to China in the 6th century, however, in China, it developed its own unique trajectory.

In the Kamakura period, the monk Yōsai, who travelled to Song China, established the Rinzai sect, and Dōgen the Sōtō sect. Zen found popularity with the *buke* warrior families in Japan, and the five great Rinzai temples of Kamakura and the five great Rinzai temples of Kyoto enjoyed great prosperity. Many Zen monks were brought over to Japan from the Song and Yuan dynasties and they established a Chinese-style Zen culture in Japan. In 1654, one such monk, Ingen, founded the *Ōbaku-shū*.

Zen culture, such as the literature of the five mountains, Zen architecture, Zen gardens, *Bokuseki* calligraphy, Zen monk portraiture, ink wash painting, the tea ceremony, flower arranging, Noh, etc. became core features of Japan's culture in the Middle Ages and we can learn about Japan's cultural interactions with China through Zen.

The thought and culture of Zen became well-known abroad due to the English publications of, and lectures given by, Suzuki Daisetsu (1870–1966). (Tr. M. Winchester)

心のルーツを探る

　日本人の心のルーツを探ることは、日本の文化の特徴あるいは本質を追求することです。これは当然の問題のようですが、じつは、特殊な問題の立て方なのです。というのも、ルーツを考えるためには、それから始まる日本というものが、時代をこえて、現在に至るまで一貫して存在している、ということを前提にしなくてはなりません。和辻哲郎の尊皇思想や柳田国男の祖先崇拝は、そのような一貫するものを捉えようとする試みの典型です。

　しかし、日本だけでなく、すべて国家というものは、時代によって大きくその姿を変えます。大和朝廷が成立した時点においては、その王権は畿内を中心としたもので、東北、東日本はまだ王権の範囲に入ってはいません。九州には、まだ王権に服属していない人々が数多く存在していました。『源氏物語』が成立したとき、平安時代の貴族にとって、東国の人々は支配の対象であって、自分たちと同じ文化に属している人間とは思えなかったでしょう。

　仏教や儒教など、外来の思想を重視していた人々にとっては、日本のルーツなどというものは、そもそも評価すべき対象ではありませんでした。日本には固有の文化があるという考え方は、長い間、あまり主張されず、江戸時代後期に国学が生まれてから徐々に意識されるようになったのです。明治以降、天皇を中心とする国家としての日本が成立すると、それを超歴史的な存在と考える思想が登場します。

　国家や民族は、時代によって変化するものです。ルーツに始まる普遍の本質は、思想的な虚構にすぎません。それが、現在の文化を決定するものではありません。その国の文化とは、人々が自分たちの時代の現実を踏まえて、未来にどのような社会を作ろうとするのかという目標によって決まるものなのです。　　　（窪田高明）

Searching for the Roots of Japanese *Kokoro*

Searching for the roots of the Japanese people's *kokoro* (heart, mind, mentality) would appear to mean to pursue the unique features or essence of Japanese culture. This is surely self-evident. However, in fact, it is a very particular way of posing a question. This is because, in order to think about these roots, we have to work on the premise that the Japan that springs from them has existed intact and consistently throughout the ages, right up until the present day. Watsuji Tetsurō's philosophy of 'reverence for the Emperor' and Yanagita Kunio's writings on 'ancestor worship' are typical attempts to try and grasp this consistency.

All states change in appearance over time. At the time of the Yamato Court, Imperial authority was centered on the capital region. That authority still did not rule Tōhoku and Eastern Japan. There were also many people in Kyūshū who did not fall under that authority. At the time when *The Tale of Genji* was being compiled, the nobles of the Heian period thought of the people in the East as subject to their control. They did not think of them as people who belonged to the same culture as themselves.

For people who treasured the originally foreign philosophies of Buddhism and Confucianism, the roots of Japan were not necessarily something to be valued. The idea that Japan had a unique culture of its own was not put forward for a long time and it was only with the emergence of National Learning (*kokugaku*) in the late Edo period that people began to become aware of it. After the Meiji period, when Japan was established as a state with the Emperor at its center, philosophies appeared that considered the roots of Japan as something supra-historical.

States and peoples change with the times. Roots that exist as universal essences are philosophically speaking nothing more than fictitious and imaginary. They do not determine contemporary culture. A country's culture is determined by how its people grasp a sense of their own time and what kind of society they aim to make in the future.

(Tr. M. Winchester)

❖日本の世界文化遺産❖

❻ 嚴島神社
Itsukushima Shinto Shrine

《自然とともにあり続ける朱丹(しゅたん)の神殿》

　海上にそびえたつ朱塗りの大鳥居が印象的な嚴島神社は、その美しい建物群だけではなく、前景には瀬戸内海、背景には神の山とされる瀰山(みせん)を配し、見事な自然と文化の調和を表現しています。世界遺産としてもその価値を評価されて、周辺の自然地域も含めて登録されました。

【所在地】広島県　【登録年】1996年
【写　真】嚴島神社社殿大鳥居（提供：廿日市市）

歴史の中の人と都市

People and Cities in History

7 | 歴史の中の人と都市

【公家】

　公家とは、前近代において天皇、朝廷に直接仕えていた貴族集団で、その身分が確立した10世紀（平安時代）から19世紀（江戸時代）まで、約800年にわたり特権階級として、京都に存続し続けました。

　12世紀前半、武士勢力が新しい公権力を樹立し、武家と呼ばれるに伴い、公家は朝廷の宮人、特に上層の廷臣の総称となりました。最高の家格は摂関家で、摂政・関白を歴任し、朝政を牛耳っていました。

　江戸時代末期（幕末）には、公家は138家がありましたが、明治維新を迎えると、東京遷都によって、事実上、公家社会は解体され、東京に移住させられました。そして、公家のほとんどは華族へ移行することによって、その身分は消滅しました。

　公家は、平安時代には国風文化と呼ばれる『源氏物語』、『古今和歌集』、寝殿造に代表される王朝文化を開花させ、また、現代に通じる雅楽・和歌・茶道といった伝統文化の発展にも寄与しました。

公家の宮廷服　シーボルト『NIPPON』（神田外語大学附属図書館所蔵）

【武士】

　武士とは、剣術・弓術・馬術などの武芸に秀でた戦闘集団です。平安時代から江戸時代まで、約700年の長きにわたって朝廷に仕え、鎌倉時代以降は幕末まで、武士は日本の支配者でした。

　武士は当初、天皇・貴族の警護や紛争の鎮圧を任されていましたが、その軍事力を武器に台頭し、貴族支配の社会を覆しました。そして、朝廷を傀儡として維持したまま、武家政権（幕府）を確立し、中世社会を主導しました。

武士の礼装　シーボルト『NIPPON』（神田外語大学附属図書館所蔵）

Kuge

The Kuge were an aristocratic class that served the Emperor and the Imperial Court during the pre-modern period. They continued to exist in Kyoto as a special class for around 800 years. They existed from the establishment of the status in the 10th century (Heian period) to the 19th century (Edo period).

Warrior forces in the early 12th century established a new public authority: the Buke. Kuge became the generic name for palace officials and other higher-classed courtiers. The highest-ranking Kuge families became regent houses and dominated court politics by serving as regents and chief councilors to the Emperor.

In the late Edo period (the *bakumatsu*) there were 138 Kuge houses; however, after the Meiji Restoration, Kuge society was for all purposes disbanded as the capital was relocated to Tokyo. The majority of Kuge families were transferred to the status of nobles (*kazoku*) and the Kuge status itself disappeared.

The Kuge were responsible for the development of the courtly culture of the Heian period known as *kokufū* of which *The Tale of Genji*, the *Kokin Wakashū* and *Shinden-zukuri* architecture are all representative. They also contributed to the development of traditional culture such as *gagaku* music, Waka poetry and Sadō (the tea ceremony), which continue to this day.

Bushi

The Bushi (often known as Samurai) were a martial population that excelled in the fighting arts, such as fencing (*kenjutsu*), archery (*kyūjutsu*) and horsemanship (*bajutsu*). From the Heian period to the Edo period the Bushi served the Imperial Court for around 700 years, and from the Kamakura period until the late Edo period they were the rulers of Japan.

The Bushi were initially charged with the protection of, and suppression of conflict among, the Emperor and the aristocratic classes. However, with their increasing military strength, the Bushi overturned society based upon aristocratic rule. While maintaining the symbolic value of the court, they established military government (*bakufu*) and were the leaders of Japanese

新渡戸稲造『武士道』初版（写真提供：盛岡市先人記念館）

　その後、武士は近世の終わりである幕末まで、日本の歴史を牽引する中心的存在であり続けました。近代に入ると、武士の身分は消滅したものの、士族として、多くが参画する近代政府、すなわち明治国家を誕生させました。

　その後、武士道という武士を律した概念が、国民道徳として引き継がれました。例えば、忠節・信義・廉恥・名誉・質素・倹約などを重視することが求められたのです。また海外にも、新渡戸稲造の『武士道』を通じて、広く紹介されました。

【忍者】

『ニンジャⅡ 修羅の章』（アメリカ映画，1983）

　忍者とは、鎌倉時代から江戸時代にわたって、中でも戦国時代を中心に、通常の武士とは異なり、歴史の裏舞台で活躍した戦闘集団です。特に、女性の忍者は「くノ一」と呼ばれました。

　忍者は、主として諜報活動、破壊工作、ゲリラ戦、暗殺などを生業として、戦国大名などに仕えました。特に有名なのは、徳川家康に仕えた甲賀と伊賀の忍者です。実在の忍者として、最も名を馳せたのは伊賀の服部半蔵です。

　忍者が修行で会得し、諜報活動などに活かしたものが忍術です。謀術、水術、火術、隠法など多岐にわたりました。また、手裏剣、鎌、隠し武器などの忍具を用いました。

　忍者という呼称は、戦後に一般的となったもので、地方によっては、乱破（らっぱ）、突破（とっぱ）、草、軒猿（のきざる）などと呼ばれていました。また、海外では80年代にニンジャムービーなどが流行し、それ以降、忍者は日本文化を代表する1つとなっています。

（町田明広）

medieval society.

Until the end of the early modern period, that is to say the *bakumatsu*, the Bushi were the central presence steering the direction of Japan's history. Despite the Bushi status being abolished in the modern era, many former Bushi participated in Japan's modern government and helped give birth to the Meiji state.

The concept of Bushidō, which had governed Bushi behavior, was later inherited as a form of national ethics: for example, in the importance given to loyalty, fidelity, shame, honor, frugality and thrift. Nitobe Inazō introduced the concept to English-language speakers in his book, *Bushido*.

Ninja

Ninja were a martial population, different from normal Bushi, which existed from the Kamakura period to the Edo period, and who were most active during the Sengoku period. They operated in the background of mainstream history. Female ninja were known as *kunoichi*.

Ninja served warring *daimyō*, among others, with their skills in espionage, sabotage, guerilla warfare and assassination. Particularly famous are the ninja from Koga and Iga that served Tokugawa Ieyasu. The name Hattori Hanzō of Iga has most prominence as a real historical ninja.

Ninjutsu is the name given to the skills of the ninja, which they gained through training. These skills were wide-ranging and included espionage, water skills, fire skills and concealment. They also used *shuriken*, sickles and hidden weapons among their other ninja implements.

After WWII, ninja became a generic term for those engaged in these activities; however, depending on the region, ninja were variously known as *rappa* (roughnecks), *toppa* (ruffians), *kusa* (grass) and *nokizaru* (eave monkeys) among others. In the 1980s a ninja movie boom occurred that led to ninja becoming a representative figure of Japanese culture.　(Tr. M. Winchester)

【奈良】

　奈良は、710年に中国の長安を模した平城京（奈良）として造営され、それ以降の74年間、日本の都として、政治・経済の中心でした。この間を、奈良時代と呼んでいます。

　日本は律令国家として完成期にあり、また、遣唐使を度々派遣して大陸の文物を導入しました。シルクロードの終着点として、奈良では国際的で仏教色豊かな天平文化が花開き、荘厳な大伽藍が建ち並ぶ都として、数々の貴重な文化財が創り出されました。

平城宮跡太極殿（奈良）
（写真提供：奈良市観光協会）

　天平文化は、聖武天皇の時代に最盛期を迎え、奈良に東大寺、全国に国分寺などが建てられました。また、国内最古の『古事記』『日本書紀』『万葉集』などの史書・歌集も、このころ編纂されました。

　太平洋戦争中、奈良は京都とともに大規模な空襲を受けていません。そのため、多くの文化遺産が存在し、現在も国際的な観光都市として、国内外から多数の観光客が訪れている日本有数の文化都市です。

【京都】

　京都は、794年に平安京として造営され、1868年に東京に遷都するまで、天皇が居所をおいた千年の都です。平安時代と室町時代（室町幕府）には、政治、経済、文化の中心地でした。

　鎌倉時代、戦国時代、安土桃山時代、幕末といった武家政権の時代でも、日本の政治の中心の1つとして、大きな役割を果たしました。

清水寺（京都）

　京都には、太平洋戦争の戦災被害を免れた神社仏閣、史跡、町並みが数多く存在し、その代表が世界

Nara

The city of Nara was established in 710 as Heijō-kyō and was modeled on the Chinese city of Chang'an (Xi'an). For 74 years it operated as the capital of Japan and the center of Japan's politics and economy. This period is known as the Nara period.

The Nara period marks the completion of Japan as a *Ritsuryō* state and many goods from the continent were introduced to Japan through the frequent dispatch of envoys. As the final destination on the Silk Road trading route, a rich culture, known as *Tempyō*, with an international Buddhist flavor, blossomed in Nara, with important Buddhist temple halls being built alongside many other valuable cultural assets.

Tempyō culture reached its prime under the reign of Emperor Shōmu. In Nara the great temple of Tōdai-ji was built and *kokubunji*, or provincial Buddhist temples, were established across the country. Japan's oldest historical and literary works, the *Kojiki*, *Nihon Shoki* and *Man'yōshū* were also compiled at this time.

During the Pacific War, Nara, like Kyoto, did not undergo large scale aerial bombing and for this reason it is one of Japan's leading cities of culture in which many cultural assets remain. As an international tourist city, many visitors from around the world travel to Nara each year.

Kyoto

Kyoto was founded as Heian-kyō in 794 and for a thousand years was the location of the Emperor's residence until the relocation of the capital to Tokyo in 1868. During the Heian and Muromachi periods, Kyoto was the center of Japan's politics, economy and culture.

Kyoto remained a center of Japanese politics and played a vital role in Japan's history even during the Kamakura, Sengoku and Azuchi-Momoyama, and the late Edo periods, when Japan was ruled by martial family (*buke*) regimes.

In Kyoto there are many shrines and temples, as well as other historical sites and streets that escaped damage during the Pacific War. Many of these sites have been designated World

狂言『棒縛』上演の様子（写真提供：和泉流宗家）

遺産に指定される文化遺産群です。能・狂言・茶道といった伝統文化、祇園祭といった祭り文化も魅力的で、国内外の多くの観光客を引き寄せています。

また、食文化も豊かであり、京野菜（聖護院かぶ・九条ねぎ・壬生菜（みぶな））、豆腐・湯葉、京漬物、おばんざい、そして伏見の酒などが代表的なものです。

英国 Wanderlust 誌の読者投票において、日本を代表する古都・京都は、2018年度ベストシティランキングで世界1位に輝いています。世界を代表する大観光都市であることが分かります。

【江戸】

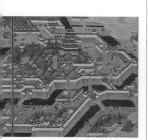

江戸城（国立歴史民俗博物館所蔵）

　江戸は、日本の首都東京の旧称であり、1603年から1867年まで続いた江戸時代に幕府が置かれて日本の政治の中心地（行政首都）として発展しました。

　江戸は、幕府の行政機構の所在地であると同時に、徳川将軍も天領と呼ばれる直轄地を支配しており、最大諸侯である徳川家の城下町でもありました。

　幕府は、参勤交代制度によって、大名を定期的に江戸に出仕させたため、一躍大消費地となり、武士階級だけでなく、士農工商と呼ばれた庶民層も流入し、人口100万人を超えた当時世界一の大都市でした。

　江戸文化は現代に通じるもが多く見られますが、その担い手の中心は台頭著しかった商人層でした。狂歌・川柳、浮世絵・錦絵、歌舞伎・浄瑠璃や、蒔絵などの工芸品などが代表的なものです。

　中でも浮世絵や工芸品は、ヨーロッパにもたらされ、ジャポニスムという日本趣味の潮流を生み出しました。例えば、ゴッホ・モネ・ドガを初めとした画家たちに大きな影響を与えました。　　　　　（町田明広）

Heritage Sites. Traditional culture such as Noh, Kyōgen and Sadō (the tea ceremony), as well as festivals such as the Gion Festival remain fascinating and attract tourists from all over the world.

Kyoto also enjoys an abundant cuisine, of which Kyoto vegetables (Shōgoin turnip, Kujō green onions, *mibuna* wild mustard leaves), *tofu*, *yuba*, Kyoto-style pickles, *obanzai* and *sake* from Fushimi are representative.

In a reader's poll taken by the British magazine *Wanderlust* in 2018, Kyoto was chosen as the world's number one city to visit. It is one of the world's representative great tourist cities.

Edo

Edo is the old name for Japan's present capital city of Tokyo. It developed during the Edo period from 1603 to 1867 as Japan's administrative capital. Edo was the center of Japan's politics and the site of the *Bakufu* (Togugawa government).

As well as being the location of the administrative organizations of the *Bakufu*, Edo provided the site from which direct control over regional fiefdoms by the Tokugawa Shogunate took place under a system known as *Tenryō*. Edo was also the location of the largest Tokugawa castle.

Under the *sankin-kōtai* system, the *Bakufu* required regional *Daimyō* to regularly travel to Edo. This meant that the city suddenly became a center for consumption. Not only the warrior class, but also common people under the 'four occupations' social class structure, flowed into the city making it one of the largest cities in the world with over a million people.

There are many elements of Edo culture that still exist today. The innovators of much Edo culture were the members of the newly-emerged merchant class of the period. *Kyōka* and *senryū* poems, *ukiyoe*, woodblock prints, *Kabuki*, *jōruri* music, *maki-e* lacquer ware are all representative of Edo culture.

Ukiyoe and other handicrafts were introduced to Europe and gave birth to the artistic movement inspired by an interest in things Japanese known as *Japonisme*. In particular, they had a significant influence on artists such as van Gogh, Monet and Degas. (Tr. M. Winchester)

日本の都市とコミュニティの歴史

　工業化以前、日本の人口の大半は農業に従事していました。稲作農業の形態上、家族の規模は今よりも大きく、相互協力が必須でした。近世初期にはある程度の工業化が進み、その結果、都市部の労働力を利用した会社のようなものも登場します。都市部は人も住居も混み合った状態だったため、火災や病気などのリスクも高まりましたが、衛生状態は良好でした。当時の日本の都市はその当時の西欧の都市よりも概して清潔だったと言われています。

　19世紀半ば以降、工業化の波を受けて日本のコミュニティは大きく形を変えてきます。男性も女性も仕事を求めて大都市に集まり、若者は職場や住居単位でまとまり新しい都市文化を作っていきました。当時の都市部の家族は大体2世代で構成され、子どもの数も少なめなのが特徴でした。東京や大阪などの大都市は、自分たちのふるさとに愛着を残した労働者を大量に中に抱えながら、新しい日本社会のシンボルとなっていきます。

　第二次世界大戦中に生活物資の配給や空襲時の消火活動を担った町内会は、後に自治会として発展していきます。戦後の日本では都市化が一層進み、核家族が標準となり、集合住宅に住む家族が増え、家電製品の発達によって高い生活水準が実現できるようになりました。またそれぞれの地域社会では行事などを行う上で女性たちが重要な役割を果たしましたが、キャリアよりも子どもや地域社会への貢献を女性に求める傾向は、今でも残っています。

　1989年のバブル経済崩壊後、雇用が減少したため仕事を求めて移動する家族もいました。しかし、未だ雇用の多くは世界で最も人口の多い首都である東京に集中しています。少子高齢化と過疎化は、現代日本のコミュニティが直面する問題です。オンラインコミュニティも急速に成長し、今日の社会の人々にとっての支えとなっています。

（亀井ダイチ・アンドリュー）

Cities and Communities in Japanese History

In pre-industrial Japan, most of the population was engaged in farming. Peasant families tended to be large, and rural communities valued cooperation because rice cultivation was labor-intensive.

By the early modern era there was a degree of protoindustrialization, resulting in the development of quasi-companies that employed an urban workforce. Life in the cities was cramped with limited living space, increasing the risk of fire and disease, but good hygiene was valued, and generally cities were cleaner than in the West at the time.

Industrialization from the mid-nineteenth century had a dramatic impact on communities. Men and women flocked into large cities to work in modern industries. Young people were united by where they lived and worked in the city, and developed a new urban culture. Urban families were usually two-generation ones with smaller numbers of children than in the countryside. Tokyo and Osaka, with their large urban workforces and national companies, became symbols of a new Japanese national community while employing many workers who retained an attachment to their rural hometowns (*furusato*).

During the Second World War, local Japanese communities worked together to distribute necessities or fight fires during air raids. These loose groups later evolved into today's neighborhood associations. Urbanization intensified in the postwar era, the nuclear family became the norm, and many families lived in apartment buildings. Modern appliances also enabled a higher standard of living. In each local community women played an important role managing local events, but the expectation that they prioritize children and community over careers persisted.

The collapse of the bubble economy in 1989 led to fewer job options and necessitated people moving their families in pursuit of work. Nevertheless, most jobs remain concentrated in Tokyo, the most populous metropolitan area in the world. The aging population, low birth rate, and emptying countryside are all issues faced by contemporary Japanese communities. Online communities have also grown rapidly and become a major source of support for people in society today. (A. T. Kamei-Dyche)

❖日本の世界文化遺産❖

❼ 古都奈良の文化財
Historic Monuments of Ancient Nara

《平城遷都1300年の文化を伝える古都》

　8世紀に日本に伝わり、その後独自の発展をとげた仏教建築群から代表として8つの物件が世界文化遺産に登録されました。それぞれの建築物は、神道や仏教など日本の宗教空間の特徴を見事に表わしています。奈良では今日でもこれらの建物を活用して宗教儀礼や行事がさかんに行われ、住民の生活や精神の中に文化として生き続けています。

【所在地】奈良県　【登録年】1998年
【写　真】興福寺　東金堂と五重塔（提供：奈良市観光協会）

8

文字文化の変遷

Transitions in Written Culture

8｜文字文化の変遷

【漢字】

漢字とカタカナで表記されたベリッツ『日本語教科書ヨヲロッパ版』（1909）（神田外語大学附属図書館所蔵）

日本語のローマ字普及のために書かれた岡倉由三郎『ローマ字の話』（1946）（神田外語大学附属図書館所蔵）

　現代日本語の表記には通常、漢字とカタカナと平仮名が使用されます。"Kandagaigodaigaku e iku niwa kaihinmakuhari eki kara basu ni nori masu"と話すことができても、漢字、カタカナ、平仮名が読めなければ、日本で生活するのは不便です。

　「なぜ日本人は三種類もの文字を使って日本語を表記しているのですか」。はじめて日本語を学ぶ外国人の中には、不思議に思い、この質問を日本人にぶつける人が多いはずです。ところが、たいていの日本人は答えるのに困ります。「だってこれが一番便利だから」と開き直る人もいるでしょう。

　「三種類の文字を学べば、日本での生活が便利になるだけではありません。文字が三種類もあること自体が日本文化の歴史的所産なのです。日本の文化と歴史を学ぶためにも、頑張ってください」と先生のように答える人もいるでしょう。

　議論が白熱すれば、「えっ、とんでもない。いつまでもそんなこと言ってるから、ネット世界でも日本語はいつまでたってもマイナー。簡単なアルファベット（ローマ字）表記に統一し、文字障壁をなくせば、バリアフリー。日常の日本語は世界中に広がり、日本文化もグローバル化します」という主張も生まれます。「日本の文化と歴史、日本の文化遺産を犠牲にするグローバル化には大反対です。牛肉やワインなどのモノはともかく、三種類の文字については譲れません。漢字は紀元3世紀ごろに中国から導入し、音訓をつけて日本語化し、9世紀初めにカタカナ、ついで、ひらがなを発明して、豊かな表記システムを作ってきたのです」との反論もあるでしょう。

Chinese characters

Contemporary Japanese makes use of three types of characters for writing: Chinese characters (*kanji*), *katakana*, and *hiragana*. Even if we can pronounce a sentence like "*kandagaigodaigaku e iku niwa kaihinmakuhari eki kara basu ni nori masu*," for somebody who cannot read *kanji*, *katakana* and *hiragana* living in Japan can be really inconvenient.

Among foreigners who start studying Japanese there are some who find this fact surprising and they ask Japanese people "Why do you use three different types of characters for writing in Japanese?" And most Japanese people are at a loss and do not know how to answer. Some of them might even retort "Because this is the most convenient way!"

Others might reply like a teacher would: "Learning the three types of characters does not necessarily mean that your life in Japan will be easier. The very fact that all these characters exist is a historical product of Japanese culture. Do your best to learn Japanese culture and history as well!"

If the discussion heats up, one might even hear an opinion such as "Unbelievable! If you continue to say things like that, Japanese will remain forever a minor language on the internet. If you remove the barrier that is the writing system by switching to Roman letters, then it would be much more easily accessible. Japanese language would then spread all over the world, and Japanese culture would become more global." On the other hand, there might be counter arguments like "I strongly oppose globalization if it means sacrificing Japanese history and the cultural heritage. I have nothing against items such as beef or wine, but I cannot yield when it comes to the three types of characters. Japanese people have created a very rich writing system, which started with the adoption of *kanji* from China in the 3rd century. They were Japanized through the introduction of *kun* readings, then *katakana* was developed in the 9th century, and *hiragana* followed later on."

8｜文字文化の変遷

カタカナによる第三期国定教科書『尋常小学国語読本』巻一（ハナ・ハト読本、1917）（東書文庫所蔵）

【カタカナ】

1904年から1947年のまで、日本の小学校1年生が初めて習う文字はカタカナでした。「ハナ　ハト　マメ　マス」で始まる教科書（1916-1932使用）は今でも有名です。

カタカナが平仮名よりも直線的で書きやすく教えやすいという事情もありますが、政府の公式な文章は明治維新（1868年）以来、漢字カタカナ交じりだったことも関係しています。一方、明治維新後に発達した新聞や雑誌は早くから漢字平仮名交じり文が中心でした。漢字カタカナ交じり文は明治維新以前、支配層あるいは男性が独占していた漢文（漢字だけで表記する文章）の読み方をもとに生まれたのです。

【平仮名】

平仮名による最後の国定教科書『こくご　一』（よいこ読本、1947）（東書文庫所蔵）

1948年から現在まで、日本の小学校1年生が最初に教科書で習う文字は平仮名です。カタカナは漢文の読み方を示す記号が起源です。平仮名は女性のために特定の漢字から作られたので、女文字とも呼ばれ、女性は平仮名だけで手紙や和歌を書きました。男性も和歌は平仮名ばかりで書きました。

1872年に小学校制度が導入されるまで、日本の子どもたちが最初に文字を習った学校は「寺子屋」とよばれ、そこでは男の子も女の子も最初は平仮名を学びました。

現代日本語の表記は、外来語にはカタカナを使用しますが、歴史的には日本の女性文化（平仮名）と男性文化（漢字）の融合したものといえます。

（松田清）

Katakana

From 1904 to 1947, the first set of characters that first-year Japanese elementary school students learned was *katakana*. A textbook called *"hana hato mame masu"* (after the first line of the first volume), which was used between 1916 and 1932, is still famous today.

There are two reasons for this: firstly, *katakana* uses simple, straight lines and is therefore easier to write and easier to teach; secondly, all official documents after the Meiji Restoration of 1868 were written in a mixture of *kanji* and *katakana*. Later on during the Meiji period, as newspapers and magazines started to spread, they used from the beginning a mixture of *kanji* and *hiragana*. The *kanji* and *katakana* mixed style of writing originated before the Meiji period, when the ruling class — especially men — was the only one familiar with *kanbun* (a type of text written exclusively in Chinese characters) and they began using *katakana* to render some of the readings.

Hiragana

From 1948 up to the present day, the first set of characters that first-year Japanese elementary school students learn has been *hiragana*. *Katakana* characters were originally used as symbols to mark the reading of *kanji* in *kanbun* texts, whereas *hiragana* were derived from *kanji* to be used by women. In the beginning, they were called *onna moji* ("letters for women"), as women wrote letters or poems by using *hiragana* exclusively. Sometimes, men also wrote poems only in *hiragana*.

Before the modern elementary school system was introduced in 1872, children had been learning how to write in facilities called *terakoya*. There, too, the first set of characters they studied was *hiragana*.

In contemporary Japanese, *katakana* characters are used for *gairaigo* (words borrowed from other languages), but it can be said that, historically, they represent the fusion between women's culture (*hiragana*) and men's culture (*kanji*). (Tr. R. Paşca)

8 | 文字文化の変遷

【書道】

　書道は毛筆と墨で文字を書く伝統芸術です。パソコンが公私の生活に不可欠となった現代日本社会でも、幅広く学ばれています。書道は中国では書法といい、書道とはいいません。書道、茶道、華道（生け花）というように、日本の伝統文化はしばしば「道」の字で終わります。日本人は分野を問わず、一筋の道を極めることに美的あるいは道徳的な価値を見い出しているようです。

　漢字が日本に渡来して以来、日本の書道は王羲之（303-361）などの中国の著名な能書家の文字を手本にしました。また、6世紀半ばに仏教が伝来すると、漢訳の経典を筆写する写経が盛んに行われ、やがて信仰と結びつきました。9世紀には空海（774-835）、嵯峨天皇（786-842）、橘 逸勢（？-842）の能書家が現れ、「三筆」と呼ばれました。『古今和歌集』（905）と『土佐日記』（935年頃）によって、平仮名の地位が確立し、漢字とともに平仮名も書道の対象になりました。

　書道が民衆の生活の中に入ったのは、庶民教育機関の寺子屋が普及しはじめた17世紀からでした。寺子屋では読み書きそろばんが教えられましたが、子どもたちは毛筆と墨を用いて、手本をひたすら反復書写する「手習い」によって、読み書きを習得しました。「手習い」は平仮名の「いろは四十七文字」から始まりました。

『土左日記』（大阪青山歴史文学博物館所蔵）

K. Florenz, *Terakoya*. Tokyo, 1900.（神田外語大学附属図書館所蔵）

【いろはかるた】

　「いろは四十七文字」とは、10世紀末頃までさか

Shodō

Shodō is the traditional Japanese art of writing characters with a brush and an ink stick. It is still widely appreciated even in contemporary Japan, in an age when computers have become an indispensable element in daily life. It is called *shūfǎ* in Chinese, which literally means "the method of writing". In Japanese traditional culture, there are many arts which are referred to as "ways", such as Shodō, Sadō ("the way of tea"), and Kadō (*ikebana*, or "the way of flowers"). The reason is that Japanese people attach both aesthetic and moral values to the idea of concentrating on only one practice, irrespective of the field.

After Chinese characters were borrowed in Japanese, Shodō practitioners initially used as models works by famous Chinese calligraphers such as Wang Xizhi (303–361). Later, with the advent of Buddhism in the 6th century, the practice of copying sutras by hand (*shakyō*) spread, and Shodō was thus connected to religious beliefs. In the 9th century, famous Japanese calligraphers became prominent, such as the monk Kūkai (774–835), Emperor Saga (786–842) and Tachibana no Hayanari (?–842), who were called "the three masters of the brush." The use of *hiragana* was established through the publication of works like *Kokinwakashū* (905) and *The Tosa Diary* (around 935), and thus hiragana became an object for Shodō alongside ideographs.

Shodō became a part of the daily life of the population after the 17th century, with the spread of the educational institutions known as *terakoya*. Reading, writing and calculus were taught in the *terakoya*, where children learned how to read and write by copying texts by hand using brushes and ink sticks. They began by learning the 47 *hiragana* characters in the *iroha* order.

Iroha playing cards

The 47 *iroha* refers to a traditional poem which dates back to

のぼる古歌「いろはにほへと　ちりぬるを　わかよたれそ　つねならむ　うゐのおくやま　けふこえて　あさきゆめみし　ゑひもせす」を指します。一文字も重ならないこの古歌は仏教の無常観を表わしているとされます。この文字の順序は「いろは順」と呼ばれ、19世紀末まで、辞書の見出し語の排列や番号付けに使用されました。

「いろはかるた」は、最初の文字によって相互に異なることわざを47種類あつめ、読み札47枚と取り札47枚を1組としたものです。「かるた」はポルトガル語のcartaに由来します。読み手がことわざを読み上げるたびに、取り手が該当する札を取り合います。同じ「い」で始まることわざでも、関東では「犬も歩けば棒に当たる」、関西では「一寸先は闇」が使われるなど、地方ごとに様々な「いろはかるた」が作られました。

【『百人一首』】

『百人一首』は、歌人藤原定家（1162–1241）が1首ずつ100人の歌人のすぐれた和歌を選んだ歌集です。『万葉集』（8世紀後半）や『古今和歌集』（905）に始まる和歌文学の中でもっとも親しまれています。

最初の歌は天智天皇（626–672）の「秋の田のかりほの庵の苫をあらみ（上の句）　わが衣手は露にぬれつつ（下の句）」です。100首の上下の句を記した読み札100枚と下の句のみを記した取り札100枚を1組みとして行うゲームも「百人一首」と呼ばれ、今も盛んに行われています。小さいときに暗誦できれば、最初は意味も分かりませんが、生涯この文学的なゲームを楽しむことができます。

（松田清）

『開化百人一首』（1907頃）（神田外語大学附属図書館所蔵）

approximately the end of the 10th century, in which the first line in Japanese starts with the sequence *i-ro-ha*: "Although its scent still lingers on / the form of a flower has scattered away / For whom will the glory / of this world remain unchanged? / Arriving today at the yonder side / of the deep mountains of evanescent existence / We shall never allow ourselves to drift away / intoxicated, in the world of shallow dreams" (tr. by Ryūichi Abe). The poem, which contains each character of the *hiragana* syllabary only once, is said to be an expression of the notion of transience in Buddhism. Until the end of the 19th century, the sequence *i-ro-ha* was used for ordering dictionary entries or other itemized lists.

The *iroha karuta* is a set of playing cards consisting of 47 *yomifuda* and 47 *torifuda*, with a proverb written on each *yomifuda* that starts with the *kana* displayed on the *torifuda*. The term *karuta* derives from the Portuguese *carta* and refers to playing cards. Each time the judge reads out the proverb on a card, the players compete trying to be the first to get the corresponding *torifuda*. There are many local variations to the *iroha karuta*, with different proverbs being used, for example, for the same *kana* in the Kantō and Kansai areas.

Hyakunin isshu

Hyakunin isshu is a classical anthology of one hundred poems by one hundred poets, compiled by Fujiwara no Teika (1162-1241). It is the most widely appreciated collection in the whole tradition of *waka* poetry, that started with *Man'yōshū* (second half of the 8th century) and *Kokinwakashū* (905).

The first poem included is "Because of the coarseness of the rush-mat / Of the temporary-hut / Where the rice of autumn harvest is / As far as my sleeve is concerned / They are becoming wet with dew (or tears)." (tr. by MacCauley), written by Emperor Tenji (626-672). There is also a game called *Hyakunin isshu* consisting of 100 *yomifuda* which contain the whole poem, and 100 corresponding *torifuda* which contain only the second part, and it is still popular today. Initially, children recite the poems from memory without understanding the meaning, but they enjoy this literary game for the rest of their lives. (Tr. R. Paşca)

前後縦横〜日本語の姿〜

　日本人は日本語を用いる社会生活において、通常、姓を先に名を後にして名乗ります。自分の姓名を文字に書き記す場合も、ローマ字も含めて、姓、名の順で書くことになっています。

　ところが、明治維新（1868年）以来、最近まで、欧米文化が押し寄せるなかで、日本人はローマ字で署名する場合、欧米人にならって名を先に、姓を後に書きつづけてきました。1862年頃まで、日本人の学ぶ西欧語はほとんどオランダ語だけでしたが、署名はオランダ語式ローマ字で、例外なく、姓、名の順に堂々と書いていたことはあまり知られていません。

　オランダ語を学んでも、姓名の順を逆転せずに署名したのは、漢学中心の知的社会の中で、蘭学が補助学問として位置づけられていたからです。蘭学が勃興した18世紀半ばからは、漢学者の間で、中国風に一字姓にして署名することが流行したほどでした。

　和文にせよ漢文にせよ、和漢混淆文にせよ、毛筆と墨でもっぱら縦書きをするのは千年以上、日本人にとって自明のことでした。19世紀末ごろから、ペンとインクが普及し、知識層を中心に横書きの習慣が始まりました。しかし、印刷物は、新聞雑誌はもちろんのこと、理工系図書、英和辞典など特殊な分野を除き、圧倒的に縦書きが支配していました。

　1945年の敗戦と漢字制限、現代仮名遣いの制定など一連の国語改革、和文タイプライターの普及によって、横書きの日本語は社会の様々な分野に広がっていきました。商店の看板は戦前、寺院の扁額と同じように、縦書きで一行一字でしたが、戦後は横書きが広がり、現在では縦書きの看板はおそらく皆無でしょう。

　現代はインターネットの普及によって横書きが縦書きを駆逐する勢いです。新聞雑誌、新刊図書の印刷文化が縦書きの最後の孤塁を守っているかのようです。

（松田清）

Left, right, up, down
~ The shape of the Japanese language ~

Japanese people usually introduce themselves by saying their family name first and their given name second. In writing, too, the rule is that they should write the family name first, even when using Roman letters.

However, after the Meiji Restoration (1868) until recently, Japanese people have imitated Westerners and written their family name in the second position when using the Latin alphabet. Until around 1862 Japanese people learned only Dutch as a foreign language, but when they signed their name they always put the family name first.

The reason why they did this was that *rangaku* ("Dutch studies") was considered to be an auxiliary discipline by the intellectuals, whose main focus was *kangaku* ("Chinese studies"). During the *rangaku* boom in the second half of the 18th century, it became fashionable among *kangaku* scholars to sign their writings using only one character, in the Chinese style.

For Japanese people, to write vertically with a brush and ink stick had been an obvious thing for more than 1,000 years, whether it was a text in Japanese, in Chinese, or a mixture of the two. At the end of the 19th century, as pens and ink became widespread, the custom of writing horizontally was established due to the influence of the intellectuals. However, in the publishing industry, with the exception of special English-Japanese dictionaries or certain scientific treatises, vertical printing was still dominant, especially in newspapers and magazines.

After a set of reforms that included limitations on the number of *kanji* used and the modernization of *kana* were put into place after World War II, horizontal writing spread in many areas of Japanese society, spurred also by the use of the Japanese-style typewriter. Store signboards, for example, which prior to the war had been written vertically like the signs found in Buddhist temples, switched to horizontal writing, and nowadays it is practically impossible to find a signboard written vertically.

Today, with the spread of the internet, horizontal writing is on the verge of completely eliminating vertical writing. It seems that the last outpost for vertical writing remains the publishing industry, through newspapers, magazines, and books.   (Tr. R. Paşca)

❖日本の世界文化遺産❖

⑧ 日光の社寺
Shrines and Temples of Nikko

《自然美と人工美が融合した徳川幕府の聖地》

　古代より、男体山、女峰山を中心とした、山岳信仰の二荒山神社、江戸時代における一流の工芸技術を集めた徳川幕府の聖地・東照宮、1250年の法灯を伝えてきた輪王寺の二社一寺が世界遺産として登録されました。美しく豪華な９棟の国宝と94棟の重要文化財があり、その周辺の山林には樹齢360年を越える杉などが生えています。

【所在地】栃木県　【登録年】1999年
【写　真】日光山輪王寺大猷院本殿（提供：日光山輪王寺）

文学にみる日本
Japan as Seen through Its Literature

『伊豆の踊子』
(新潮文庫刊)

【川端康成】

　1968年に日本人で初のノーベル文学賞を受賞した川端康成は直ちに世界中で有名になりました。「新感覚派」の代表的作家としても知られており、当時の日本の文壇ではリーダー的な存在でした。三島由紀夫のような若手の作家をサポートするなど、作家の卵を発見し自立に導く才能もあったと言われています。

　代表作に『伊豆の踊子』『雪国』『千羽鶴』『古都』などがありますが、創意に満ちた作品を数多く書いています。その共通点として、人間の「悪」や「醜」を「美」に変えることができるというヒューマニスティックな見解が挙げられます。

　一方、和歌や随筆など、日本の伝統文化に深く根ざしているとされる川端の作品のスタイルは、詩的なものとして高く評価されています。そのすべての作品を貫く一番大きな筋は「日本の美」というテーマであり、ノーベル賞受賞講演でも、川端は「美しい日本の私」というタイトルで日本人の美意識を概観し、世界に紹介しました。

『雪国』
(新潮文庫刊)

【大江健三郎】

　1958年に大学在学中に最年少の23歳で芥川賞を受賞した大江健三郎は、1994年に日本人で2人目のノーベル文学賞受賞者ともなります。大江も川端康成と同様に詩的な(時には難解な)言語を用いますが、日本の伝統文化ではなく、現代の人間の、普遍的な窮状や苦しみを描いた作家として世界中で知名度が高い作家です。

　主な作品に、『飼育』『個人的な体験』『万延元年

『死者の奢り・飼育』
(新潮文庫刊)

Kawabata Yasunari

When he won the Nobel Prize for literature in 1968, Kawabata Yasunari became instantly famous worldwide. A leader-like presence on the Japanese literary scene of the time, he was also known as one of the most representative writers of the Neo-sensualist movement. He is also said to have had the gift of discovering and mentoring aspiring writers, and he supported many young authors including Mishima Yukio.

He published many original works, the most representative being *The Izu Dancer, Snow Country, Thousand Cranes* and *The Old Capital*. What all these texts have in common is an extremely humanistic view in which the evil and cruelty in human beings can be changed into beauty.

Kawabata's style is appreciated for its poetic character, which is deeply rooted in Japanese traditional literary genres such as poetry (*waka*) and essay (*zuihitsu*). One of the topics which can be found as a recurring theme in almost all his writings is the "Japanese sense of beauty". In his Nobel lecture, titled "Japan, the Beautiful and Myself", he tried to sum up the aesthetic sense of Japanese people and introduce it to the world.

Ōe Kenzaburō

Ōe Kenzaburō, the youngest recipient ever of the Akutagawa Prize at the age of 23 — in 1958, when he was still a student — is also the second Japanese writer to have received the Nobel Prize for literature, in 1994. Like Kawabata, Ōe also uses a poetic (and, at times, difficult) language, but he departs from traditional Japanese culture. He is known across the globe as an author who writes about the universal predicament and suffering of the contemporary individual.

Among his most important writings are *Prize Stock, A Personal Matter*, and *The Silent Cry*. The Nobel Prize Committee said about his works that they present an imagined

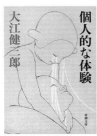

『個人的な体験』
(新潮文庫刊)

のフットボール』などがありますが、ノーベル委員会によると、大江は生命と神話が凝縮されている想像的な世界を言葉の力のみによって創りだしたと言われています。実存主義など、西洋の哲学や思想の影響も受けたと言われている大江は、想像力が現実を形成・転換することができるというスタンスで数多くの作品を書いています。さらに、小説だけでなく、エッセイやルポルタージュなども執筆している大江健三郎は活動家としても活躍しています。

【村上春樹】

『海辺のカフカ(上)』
(新潮社刊)

村上春樹は1979年に『風の歌を聴け』でデビューしましたが、1987年に発表された『ノルウェイの森』が瞬く間にベストセラーになり、村上ブームの引き金となりました。その後、村上は数多くの小説やエッセイを執筆し、現在日本国内だけでなく世界中で人気が高い作家の一人です。代表作に『羊をめぐる冒険』、『海辺のカフカ』、『1Q84』などがあります。

ノーベル文学賞の有力候補者とも見なされている村上の小説は、心に訴えかける物語であると称賛されています。初期の作風は、1995年に起きた地下鉄サリン事件や阪神・淡路大震災を契機にデタッチメントからコミットメントへと変わり、社会に無関心だった登場人物は社会問題と直面するようになります。村上作品のそういったテーマの転換も高く評価されています。

『1Q84 BOOK 1』
(新潮社刊)

村上春樹の数多くの作品は、英語やフランス語をはじめ、40か国語以上に翻訳されています。

(ロマン・パシュカ)

world in which life and myth are condensed, created only through the power of words. Ōe was influenced by Western thought and philosophy, particularly by existentialism, and he wrote many of his texts starting from the premise that imagination has the power to shape and transform reality. Apart from novels, Ōe also published many essays and reportages, and he is still quite influential as an activist.

Murakami Haruki

Murakami Haruki made his debut in 1979 with *Hear the Wind Sing*, but it was his 1987 novel *Norwegian Wood* that became an instant best-seller and triggered the so-called "Murakami boom." He has published numerous novels and essays and, currently, he is probably the most famous Japanese writer not only in Japan, but also abroad. Among his most representative works are *A Wild Sheep Chase*, *Kafka on the Shore*, and *1Q84*.

Murakami is seen as a strong candidate for the Nobel Prize, and his novels are often praised for telling stories that appeal to human emotions. After the Tokyo subway sarin attack and the Great Hanshin Earthquake of 1995, the style of his works changed from detachment to commitment, and his characters, who had been oblivious of society, now became involved and had to face various social problems. This transformation is also highly appreciated.

Many of Murakami's writings have been translated, not only into English or French, but into more than 40 languages.

(R. Paşca)

【源氏物語】

『源氏物語』は紫式部が著した長編物語です。世界初の小説とも言われている作品でもあり、通常54帖からなっているとされます。この物語は平安時代中期に書かれたものですが、その主たるモチーフは「もののあはれ」という美的理念です。「もののあはれ」とは、五感がものごとに刺激された際に生じる無常観的な情趣のことで、江戸時代の国学者本居宣長などによって提唱され、日本文化における価値観の形成に大きな影響を与えた理念です。

『源氏物語』では、主人公の光源氏を軸に平安朝の生活ぶりが詳細に描かれ、当時の貴族の文化が垣間見えるので、歴史的資料としても使われます。さらに、漫画、アニメ、音楽など、現在でも様々な分野で引用され、非常に影響力のある作品として評価され続けている日本の古典文学の代表的な存在です。英語をはじめ、フランス語、イタリア語、ロシア語など、様々な言語に翻訳されています。

【おくの細道】

松尾芭蕉（早稲田大学図書館所蔵）

松尾芭蕉（1644-1694）は日本のみならず世界中でもっとも有名な俳諧師の1人で、想像力に満ちた、芸術性の高い俳句を確立した「俳聖（はいせい）」として知られています。和歌の伝統的な風雅を知りつつも、日常を平易かつ自由に描くことが重要であると強調し、卑近な題材の中に発見された新しい美を表現するために「かるみ」という理念を提唱しました。

芭蕉によって著された『おくの細道』という紀行文は1702年に刊行されましたが、この作品も古典文学

Genji monogatari

Genji monogatari, which is sometimes considered to be the first novel in the world, is a long *monogatari* authored by Murasaki Shikibu. The story, usually divided into 54 chapters, was written around the middle of the Heian period and one of its main motifs is the aesthetic concept of *mono no aware* ("the pathos of things"). *Mono no aware* was theorized in the Edo period by *Kokugaku* scholar Motoori Norinaga, and refers to the feeling of impermanence that is born when the five senses receive stimuli from the surrounding environment. It is a concept that has had a great influence on the formation of many values prized in Japanese culture.

Focusing on the main character Hikaru Genji, *Genji monogatari* describes in detail the lifestyle at the Imperial Court during the Heian period, thus allowing the reader to catch a glimpse of the culture of the aristocracy. That is why it has also been used as a valuable resource of historical information. *Genji monogatari* is a representative work of the body of Japanese classical literature and an extremely influential writing which to this day continues to be cited and used in a variety of fields, including manga, anime, or music. It has been translated into many languages, among them English, French, Italian, and Russian.

The Narrow Road to the Deep North

Matsuo Bashō (1644-1694) is one of the most famous *haiku* poets not only in Japan, but across the globe, known as the "*haiku* saint" who established *haiku* as a highly imaginative and artistic literary form. He was well-versed in the elegance of Japanese traditional poetry, but at the same time he insisted on the importance of writing freely about ordinary life, in a plain style. He proposed the concept of *karumi* ("lightness") as a means to convey new beauty found in mundane topics.

Bashō's *Oku no hosomichi* ("The Narrow Road to the Deep North"), a prose and verse travel diary published in 1702, is considered one of the major texts of classical Japanese literature. The diary is a detailed account of the two-year journey that

の代表的なものです。芭蕉が江戸から旅立ち約2年間東北や北陸を巡ってまた江戸に帰ってくるという旅程が描かれ、中にはたくさんの俳句が詠み込まれています。「夏草や 兵(つわもの)どもが 夢のあと」はその1つの例ですが、この句にも見られるように、芭蕉が詠んだ俳句の大きな特徴として、日常的な言葉を使いながらも詩精神に富んだものであることがよく挙げられています。

【坊ちゃん】

夏目漱石
(国立国会図書館)

夏目漱石(1867-1916)は明治時代の作家ですが、日本の近代文学に非常に大きな影響を与えた人物として名高い評判を得ています。学生時代の正岡子規との出会いがきっかけで文学に興味を持つようになり、最初は俳句を学びますが、その後に小説、随筆、漢詩、評論など、様々なジャンルの作品を書きます。イギリス留学からの帰国後、東京帝国大学で英文学の講師も勤めます。

漱石の有名な中編小説の1つである『坊っちゃん』は、1906年に発表されましたが、現在でも愛読されています。その主な理由は、文章の新鮮さや奇抜さにあると言われています。ユーモアに満ちたおもしろい文体によって、生き生きとしたストーリーが展開されています。主人公の坊っちゃんは純粋な江戸っ子ですが、四国の中学校で数学教師になります。滑稽に描かれた坊っちゃんの人物像は笑いを呼びますが、その描写から明治時代の人々の日常生活や文化も垣間見ることができるところも高く評価されています。

(ロマン・パシュカ)

Bashō made from Edo through the northern regions of Tōhoku and Hokuriku and then back to Edo, sprinkled throughout with many *haiku* poems. One of the most famous examples is "The summer grasses — / Of brave soldiers' dreams / The aftermath" (trans. by D. Keene). As can be seen from this poem, the main characteristic of Bashō's *haikus* is their rich poetic spirit expressed with ordinary words.

Botchan

Natsume Sōseki (1867-1912) is a Meiji period author who is recognized as an extremely influential figure in the development of modern Japanese literature. He became interested in literature after he befriended Masaoka Shiki while still a student. He began by studying traditional poetry (*haiku*) and later on published numerous works in different genres such as novels, essays, Chinese poetry, and reviews. Upon his return from London, where he studied for several years, he became a professor in English literature at the Tokyo Imperial University.

Botchan, the novel he published in 1906, is one of his most famous works, and is still widely read and appreciated. The main reason for the short novel's popularity is probably the humorous writing style, so fresh and unconventional that it creates a very vivid story. The main character Botchan is a pure Tokyoite, but he becomes a mathematics teacher in a middle school in Shikoku. Botchan's comical image is definitely amusing, but the book is also highly appreciated for offering a glimpse into the culture and the daily life of ordinary people during the Meiji period.

(R. Paşca)

翻訳を通して世界から見た日本

　日本文学は7世紀まで遡ることができ、極めて永い歴史を誇っています。例えば、自然の豊かさや人々の喜怒哀楽などを詠んだ和歌が数多く収められている『万葉集』は8世紀後半に編纂された和歌集だといわれています。

　日本人の作家は、古代から中世にかけては中国文化や仏教、そして明治維新以降は西洋文学の影響を受けながらも創意に満ちた日本独自の、非常にレベルの高い作品を創造していきました。短歌、俳句、物語、随筆、私小説など、現代にかけて日本特有の様々なジャンルを生み出してきました。

　そして現在、そのようなオリジナリティに富んだ日本文学の作品は様々な言語に翻訳されて広く読まれ、世界的に知られるようになりました。ノーベル文学賞を受賞した川端康成や大江健三郎の作品のみならず、『源氏物語』や『方丈記』のような古典文学から三島由紀夫や村上春樹の小説まで非常に高く評価されています。日本人作家の想像力や独創性が称賛され、その文体・スタイル・内容が摂取され、世界文学に影響を与えるようになりました。

　では、文学作品を日本語から他の言語に翻訳することにはどのような意義があるのでしょうか。この問いに対して様々な回答が考えられますが、最も有力な答えとしては「日本を知ること」が挙げられるでしょう。英語、またはフランス語やドイツ語、あるいはルーマニア語やセルビア語などのようなマイナーな言語に翻訳された日本文学の作品を読むことを通して、日本国外の人々は日本という国の真の姿を垣間み、日本人が持っている価値観、自然観、死生観など、独自の思想や感性を知ることができます。そしてそれが、日本についてよりポジティヴなイメージを持つことにも繋がると思われます。「目は心の窓」と言われているように、「文学も心の窓」と言えるでしょう。

（ロマン・パシュカ）

Japan as Seen from the World through Translation

Japanese literature has a very long tradition that goes back in time as far as the 7th century. For example, the anthology *Man'yōshū*, which contains many poems on topics such as the beauty of nature or human emotions, is said to have been compiled from the second half of the 7th century to the second half of the 8th.

While being influenced by Chinese culture and by Buddhism from the classical period to the medieval period, and then by Western literature after the Meiji Restoration, Japanese writers have produced a high quality, and very original, body of work. They also created several literary genres and works that are specific to Japan, such as *tanka*, *haiku*, *monogatari*, *zuihitsu*, or *shishōsetsu* ("I novel").

Many of these original Japanese literary works have been translated into various languages, and they have come to be read and known all over the world. From the writings of Nobel prize winners like Kawabata Yasunari and Ōe Kenzaburō, to classic works like *Genji monogatari* or *Hōjōki*, or to the novels of Mishima Yukio and Murakami Haruki, Japanese literature is very highly appreciated. The creativity and imagination of Japanese writers are often praised, while the style and content of their works has been assimilated into world literature and started to influence it.

But why is it important to translate Japanese literary works into other languages? There are many possible answers to this question, but one of the most obvious is probably "to get to know Japan." By reading literary works translated into English, French, German, or even into minor languages such as Romanian or Serbian, people across the globe can catch a glimpse of Japan as it is, and they can learn about the sensibility and way of thinking of Japanese people — their values, their views on Nature or on life and death. And this can also make them have a more positive image of Japan. There is a saying that "eyes are windows to the soul," but maybe "literature too is a window to the soul."

(R. Paşca)

❖日本の世界文化遺産❖

琉球王国のグスク及び関連遺産群
Gusuku Sites and Related Properties of the Kingdom of Ryukyu

《南海に花開いた華麗な王朝文化》

　12世紀から17世紀にわたり独自の文化を築いた琉球王国の歴史は、県内に点在する9つの遺跡によって代表されます。高台にそびえる廃墟の城（グスク）はその時期の社会構造を、斎場御嶽（セーファウタキ）などの聖地は古代宗教の存続を表わしています。首里城は15世紀初頭に統一王国を築いた尚巴志によって整備され、王国の政治・行政・外交・貿易・文化の拠点となっていました。

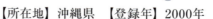

【所在地】沖縄県　【登録年】2000年
【写　真】首里城正殿（提供：首里城公園）

⟨10⟩ 芸術と感性
Art and Sensibility

【やまと絵】

　やまと絵は日本の絵という意味です。日本の古代・中世の絵画は、主題や様式、技法などを中国絵画から学ぶことにより発展したため、中国からもたらされた絵やそれらに倣って日本で描かれた絵を唐絵と呼んで珍重していました。

　平安時代前期にいたって日本的な題材による四季絵や月次絵（十二か月の風物に取材した絵）、名所絵といった主題が屏風や障子（襖障子や衝立障子）に描かれるようになり、そうした絵を唐絵に対してやまと絵と呼ぶようになりました。そして鎌倉時代に新たに宋・元の水墨画がもたらされると、従来の絵のことをやまと絵と呼ぶようになりました。

　王朝の雅な雰囲気を伝えるやまと絵は主に天皇や公家に好まれ、宮廷の絵所を中心に継承されました。室町時代に土佐を名のる絵師が絵所預の職を世襲するようになり、土佐派はやまと絵の流派として江戸時代末まで栄えました。やまと絵の伝統は現代の日本画にも直接間接の影響を与え続けています。

【絵巻】

　絵巻は横長の巻物形式の絵のことです。右から左へ両手で繰広げながら鑑賞するため、空間的表現に加えて時間的表現の効果があります。物語の絵画化に適しており、しばしば詞書と交互に配されました。中国から伝えられた形式ですが、日本でも主に中世に様々な主題の絵巻がつくられました。

　平安時代前期に物語文学が成立すると、早くから絵が添えられ、宮廷の女性たちに享受されました。

Yamato-e

Yamato-e is a term for Japanese paintings. Painting in classical and medieval Japan developed through the adoption of themes, styles, and techniques from Chinese paintings. Works imported from China or painted in imitation of Chinese paintings were called *Kara-e* ("Chinese-style painting") and long treasured.

From the early Heian period, pictures with Japanese themes — such as seasonal pictures, *tsukinami-e* (based on seasonal motifs), or famous places — came to be depicted on folding screens or paper sliding doors, and were called *Yamato-e*, to distinguish them from *Kara-e*. Following the introduction of Song- and Yuan-Dynasty ink paintings in the Kamakura period, the term broadened to also include previous Japanese-style painting.

Yamato-e were appreciated by the sovereign and courtiers in particular because they conveyed the elegant atmosphere of the court, and the art form was transmitted mainly by the Edokoro (court atelier). During the Muromachi period, a family of painters named Tosa came to inherit the post of head of the Edokoro, leading to the development of the Tosa School of *Yamato-e* which flourished until the end of the Edo period. The *Yamato-e* tradition has also exerted a considerable influence, both directly and indirectly, on much of modern Japanese art.

Emaki (Picture Scroll)

Emaki refers to rectangular illustrated scrolls. Since such scrolls are unrolled from right to left with both hands, they create not only a spatial expression but a temporal one as well. This medium is well-suited for depicting narratives, and it was frequently used to convey stories with accompanying illustrations. This art form was originally transmitted from China, but numerous picture scrolls on a variety of themes were created in Japan, particularly in the medieval era.

Not long after the development of *monogatari* (narratives/tales) literature in the early Heian period, illustrations were added to these stories and they were especially enjoyed by women of the court. Such *monogatari* picture scrolls were characterized by elaborate techniques with deep color and

物語絵巻は、つくり絵といわれる濃彩で緻密な技法と象徴的な表現に特色があり、徳川・五島本「源氏物語絵巻」(12世紀) は王朝文化の精華として知られています。他方、説話文学を題材とした説話絵巻は、話の展開を暢達な描線で活写するところに見どころがあり、多様な画風がみられます。

室町時代には歴代将軍の多くが土佐派の絵師たちに絵巻をつくらせています。武家は公家勢力への文化的対抗意識もあって唐絵を好みましたが、伝統文化の外護者にもなりました。

【琳派】

「風神雷神図屏風」尾形光琳（東京国立博物館所蔵　Image：TNM Image Archives）

琳派は近世のやまと絵の流派です。桃山時代から江戸時代初期に生きた宗達を祖とし、尾形光琳 (1658-1716)、酒井抱一 (1761-1828) によって継承されました。かれらに師弟関係はなく、先人の遺した画業に感銘をうけた私淑の系譜といわれます。宗達の描いた「風神雷神図」(建仁寺) を光琳が模写し、光琳の模写図（東京国立博物館）を抱一が模写した図（出光美術館）が現存しています。

桃山時代には乱世が終息し、王朝文化復興の気運が高まっていました。そうしたなか俵屋という絵屋を営んでいた宗達は独学でやまと絵を学び、古典文学などを主題に雅で華やかな金碧画を描きました。光琳は呉服商雁金屋の生まれで、天賦の意匠感覚をもとに宗達の装飾的な画風を発展させました。抱一は姫路藩主酒井家の次男の身分で、光琳に傾倒して自らも瀟洒な絵を描き、『光琳百図』『尾形流略印譜』を刊行して光琳を顕彰するとともに尾形流（琳派）の系譜を跡づけました。

（吉村稔子）

symbolic expression. The 12th-century *emaki* of the *Tale of Genji* (held by the Tokugawa Art Museum and the Gotoh Museum) is well-known for reflecting the glory of court culture. On the other hand, *setsuwa* picture scrolls based on *setsuwa* (folktales, anecdotes) writings are noteworthy for depicting the unfolding of the stories in facile lines. A variety of painting styles existed.

During the Muromachi period, many of the shoguns had painters of the Tosa School produce picture scrolls. Warrior families tended to prefer *Kara-e*, due to their cultural rivalry with courtiers, but they also became patrons of the traditional arts.

Rinpa School

The Rinpa School is one of the schools of *Yamato-e* (Japanese painting). It originated with Tawaraya Sōtatsu, who lived from the Momoyama through early Edo periods, and was continued by Ogata Kōrin (1658–1716) and Sakai Hōitsu (1761–1828). These figures were not linked by master-apprentice relations; rather, the lineage of the school was the product of each artist admiring the work of their predecessors. Sōtatsu's *Fūjin Raijin-zu* (Wind and Thunder Gods) was imitated by Kōrin, whose own piece was in turn copied by Hōitsu. All three works are extant today (kept at Ken'ninji Temple, Tokyo National Museum, and Idemitsu Museum of Arts, respectively).

In the Momoyama period, there was a respite from the tumultuous Sengoku era, and a revival of interest in court culture. Against this backdrop, Sōtatsu, who had been running a picture store called Tawaraya, learned Japanese painting by himself and came to paint elegant, gorgeous *kinpeki-ga* (pictures with gold backgrounds) based on classical themes and the like.

Kōrin, born to a merchant named Kariganeya, further developed Sōtatsu's decorative painting style based on his own natural sense of design. As for Hōitsu, he hailed from the Sakai *daimyō* family that ruled Himeji domain. Although he was the second son of the lord, his admiration for Kōrin led him to paint elegant pictures of his own. He published a book of prints of Kōrin's work entitled *Kōrin Hyakuzu* (A Hundred Paintings by Kōrin), to honor Kōrin, and *Ogata-ryū Ryakuin-fu* (Abbreviated Lineage of the Ogata School), to trace the lineage of the Ogata (Rinpa) School. (Tr. A. T. Kamei-Dyche)

【雅楽】

　雅楽とは、古代に宮廷で演奏された伝統音楽です。5・6世紀に中国や朝鮮半島から日本に伝わった音楽と、日本に上代から伝わる音楽や舞踏とが融合して生まれました。当初より宮廷音楽として発展し、平安時代中期に大成。朝廷の政治的権力の低下に伴って一時期衰退しましたが、絶えることなく伝承され、現在では、大規模に合奏形態で行われる音楽としては日本最古のものと認識されています。

　雅楽で用いられる楽器には、打物(うちもの)と呼ばれる打楽器（羯鼓(かっこ)、太鼓(たいこ)、大太鼓(だだいこ)、鉦鼓(しょうこ)。演奏時の指揮者的役割）、吹物(ふきもの)と呼ばれる管楽器（篳篥(ひちりき)、龍笛(りゅうてき)、笙(しょう)。旋律を担う）、弾物(ひきもの)と呼ばれる絃楽器（楽琵琶(がくびわ)、楽箏(がくそう)、和琴(わごん)。主にリズムをとる）があります。中でも和琴は日本古来のものとして、他の弾物とは区別されています。雅楽は舞楽の伴奏としても用いられていて、1955年には国の重要無形文化財の指定を受け、2009年には、ユネスコ無形文化遺産に登録されました。

管絃（写真提供：宮内庁式部職楽部）

【アイドル】

　「アイドル」とは、音楽活動やメディアを通じてファンができる若い芸能人を指します。現代のような「アイドル」が生まれたのは1970年代に入ってからです。若くて明るく、容姿に優れていることが大切で、音楽やダンスなどの才能は二の次とされます。

　人気アイドルの中には少年のみで形成されているものもありますが、主流は10代後半の少女たちです。特定のイメージが芸能プロによって作り上げられ、それを壊さないように厳しい規則が作られる場合があ

Gagaku

Gagaku refers to a form of traditional music performed at the Japanese Court in ancient times. Gagaku developed from a synthesis of ancient Japanese music and dance with music imported from China and the Korean peninsula in the 5th and 6th centuries. Gagaku developed into a distinct tradition of courtly music, and reached its zenith in the mid-Heian period. It subsequently experienced a decline as the court upon which it depended experienced a loss of political power and prestige, but was passed down until the present. Today it is recognized as Japan's oldest tradition of orchestral music.

Gagaku incorporates percussion (*uchimono*, which keep time for the performance like a conductor), wind (*fukimono*, which carry the melody) and string (*hikimono*, mainly for rhythm) instruments. Percussion instruments include *kakko* (small hourglass-shaped drum), *taiko* (drum), *dadaiko* (large drum), and *shōko* (gong, a unique metal instrument). Wind instruments commonly used are *hichiriki* (double-reed flute), *ryūteki* (transverse flute), and *shō* (reed mouth organ). String instruments include a variety of *biwa* (4-stringed lute) known as *gakubiwa, gakusō* (floor zither), and *wagon* (6-stringed zither). Among these the *wagon* is distinct because of its ancient Japanese origin.

A Gagaku performance can also be used to provide accompaniment for Bugaku (classical dance). Gagaku was designated as an Important Intangible Cultural Property in 1955, and a UNESCO Intangible Cultural Heritage in 2009.

Idols

Idols, or more specifically pop idols, are young celebrities who primarily build a fanbase through musical performance but who also participate in a wide variety of pop media such as variety shows and festive events. While celebrity performers have a long history in Japanese urban culture, the modern idol phenomenon took off in the 1970s. Young, perky and usually female, the cute appearance and style of the idol was usually just as important, if not even more so, than her talent at singing and dancing.

While there are many popular boy groups, the prevalent image is of teenage girls, and indeed the majority of idols are young women. Idols must all maintain a cute look and demeanor,

ります。恋愛禁止などはその一例です。現在、AKB48に代表されるような多人数によるアイドルグループが人気ですが、これは1990年代後半に登場したモーニング娘がその最初です。2000年に入るとアイドルとメタルの融合を目指したサブカルチャーベースのアイドル（Baby Metal）や暗黒系ユニットも誕生。また日本各地にはその地域に密着した「ご当地アイドル」なども存在しています。

【ビジュアル系】

　ビジュアル系とは、日本音楽界の様式の1つで、派手な衣装や化粧、ヘアスタイルにその特徴があります。ビクトリア朝やロココ調のファッションを真似たり光沢のある革で作られた衣装などを着用し、中性的な美しさを売りにすることが多いようです。

　「ビジュアル系」という言葉自体は、1980年代に一世を風靡したロックバンド・X Japanのキャッチコピー"Psychedelic Violence Crime of Visual Shock"から生まれました。初期のビジュアル系バンドとしてはBuck-Tick、Luna Sea、Malice Mizerなどが有名です。2000年半ばには、Dir en Grey、The Gazette、Jupiter（当初はVersailles）、Alice Nineなどの新世代ビジュアル系が出てきましたが、彼らは初期のビジュアル系よりもはるかにイメージの演出に重点をおいています。こうした傾向はビジュアル系を特徴づけるものですが、その偏りには批判も少なからずあります。バンドの中には、海外にも根強いファンを持つものもあります。　　　　　　　（亀井ダイチ・アンドリュー）

as well as a wholesome image (created by their studio) that enables them to serve as role models for children and inspire people with their upbeat and innocent character. Sometimes idols must adhere to a strict code — including, for instance, a prohibition on romantic relationships.

Large idol groups first gained significant popularity with Morning Musume in the late 1990s, but today the leading group is the ubiquitous AKB48. Alternative idol acts include BabyMetal, which dances to heavy metal music, and Necronomidol, which incorporates dark and gothic stylistics. Many local regions and even stores may develop their own idol groups.

Visual Kei

Visual kei ("visual style") is a trend in modern Japanese music that incorporates a particular focus on flamboyant costumes, make-up and complex hairstyles. It may also, but not necessarily, include an androgynous aesthetic. Elegant dresses and coats inspired by Victorian or Rococo fashion, theatrical pirate garb, or elaborate sleek leather outfits are just some of the clothing regularly worn by visual kei bands.

The term "visual kei" itself is usually seen as derived from "Psychedelic Violence Crime of Visual Shock," a slogan of hard rock/heavy metal act X Japan that had achieved breakthrough popularity in the late 1980s. Along with X Japan itself, bands associated with the style in the early years included Buck-Tick, Luna Sea, and Malice Mizer. The newer mid-2000s generation of visual kei bands includes Dir en Grey, The Gazette, Jupiter (formerly Versailles), and Alice Nine. The excessive focus on image that characterizes visual kei has, however, been criticized as the triumph of style over substance by some critics. Some visual kei bands have found overseas audiences.

(A. T. Kamei-Dyche)

ジャポニスム

　19世紀後半から20世紀初頭にかけて欧米で日本文化ブームが起こりました。1854年に日本が開国すると、日本を訪れた外交官らが日本を紹介する本を出版し、おりから欧米で開催されていた万国博覧会に日本が出展するようになると、日本文化に対する関心が高まったのです。18世紀に流行した中国趣味（シノワズリー）につづく日本趣味（ジャポネズリー）ともいわれますが、たんなる異国趣味にとどまらず、芸術家たちの創作活動に広範な影響を与えたという意味では、日本主義、フランス語でジャポニスムといいます。その影響は美術・工芸、建築・庭園から文学、演劇、服飾などに及びました。

　最も豊かな成果がみられたのは絵画の分野です。当時の西欧絵画は写真の発明もあって写実主義が衰退し、20世紀のモダニズムへ向かう転換期にありました。そうした閉塞感のなか、日本絵画によって新しいものの見方や表現の仕方が示されたのです。画家たちは、主に浮世絵の風景版画や装飾美術を通して、自然への親和的な態度や季節への鋭敏な感覚、それらを表現する俯瞰的な構図、簡潔な描線、平面的な彩色、装飾性などを学び、自らの創作に生かしてゆきました。受容の様相は様々ですが、ジェイムズ・マクニール・ホイッスラー、エドゥアール・マネから印象派・後期印象派、ナビ派、象徴主義の画家たち、グスタフ・クリムト、アンリ・マチスなどの作品が挙げられます。

　絵画における日本的手法は、西欧絵画のなかに見事に取り込まれたことにより、ことさら日本的と意識されなくなりました。戦後の東京でマチス展と宗達・光琳展とがたまたま同時に開催されたとき、マチスとの比較で宗達の近代性が再評価されたといいます。ジャポニスムは、他文化の視点から日本の伝統文化の価値に気づかせてくれたといえるでしょう。　　　　　　　　　（吉村稔子）

Japonisme

From the late 19th through early 20th centuries, Japanese culture experienced a boom in the West. Following the opening of Japan in 1854, diplomats who visited the country published books about it, while Japan's exhibitions at world's fairs in the West further increased interest in Japan. This came to be called "Japonaiserie" in the vein of the "Chinoiserie" (Chinese influence) that had been popular in the 18th century. However, this did not stop with mere exoticism, but exerted a broad influence over creative work by many artists. In this regard it was akin to "Japan-ism," and indeed became known as *Japonisme* in French. Its influence encompassed the visual arts, architecture, gardening, literature, performing arts, and fashion.

The most significant case was painting. Contemporary Western painting had witnessed a decline in realism, partly due to the development of photography, and had reached a turning point moving towards the modernism of the 20th century. In an environment where artists felt trapped, Japanese paintings introduced new perspectives and modes of expression. Primarily through the scenic prints and decorative art of *ukiyoe*, many Western painters developed an affinity for nature and a sharp sense for the seasons. They also acquired the tools necessary to convey these — comprehensive composition, simple lines, planar coloring, embellishments and so forth — and incorporated them in their work. The ways in which they adapted elements from *ukiyoe* varied significantly. Prominent examples include James McNeill Whistler, Édouard Manet, the Impressionists and Post-Impressionists, Les Nabis, the Symbolists, Gustav Klimt, and Henri Matisse.

As a result of the skillful incorporation of Japanese techniques into Western painting, the awareness of these elements as "Japanese" faded. When an exhibition on Matisse was held in postwar Tokyo at the same time as one on Tawaraya Sōtatsu and Ogata Kōrin, the modernity in Sōtatsu's work was re-evaluated through comparisons with the work of Matisse. Japonisme makes us aware of the value of traditional Japanese culture from the perspectives of other cultures. (Tr. A. T. Kamei-Dyche)

❖日本の世界文化遺産❖

❿
紀伊山地の霊場と参詣道
Sacred Sites and Piligrimage Routes in the Kii Mountain Range

《人びとの信仰の対象となった聖なる場所》

　太平洋を臨む紀伊山地に、奈良と京都をつなぐ参詣道と吉野・大峯、熊野三山、高野山という３つの霊場があります。それらは日本の自然に根づく神道と、中国と朝鮮半島から伝来した仏教の融合を示すものです。この地域は、近隣の森林環境を含め1200年以上もの間、神聖な山としてあがめられ、毎年多くの人々が巡礼のために訪れます。

【所在地】三重県・奈良県・和歌山県　【登録年】2004年
【写　真】熊野本宮大社（提供：和歌山県）

⟨11⟩ クールジャパンの系譜
A Genealogy of Cool Japan

【AKB48】

　AKB48は大勢の「少女」で構成される「実際に会いにいけるアイドル」として国民的に知られています。彼女たちとは、秋葉原の小さな劇場で毎日会えます。全国各地を廻り、ファンたちと握手をする活動もしています。彼女たちは、立候補者300人ほどからCDを購入したファンたちの投票の数で毎年順位が決められます。AKB48は100名ほどで構成され、6つの「チーム」からなり、上位7人がメディアへの頻出度が高く、16番目までが「選抜メンバー」とされます。

　彼女たちは練習を積み、互いに高め合い競争し合う関係にあります。ファンたちはその成長を見守りながら「育てる」感覚で支持しています。彼女たちは、男性にとり、擬似恋愛感情の対象にもなり、女性にとっては、憧れと共感を抱く存在でもあります。「普通の女の子たち」が披露する踊りと歌から「努力は必ず報われる」というメッセージが読み取れます。

【ヤンキー】

"かわいい"を派手な化粧で自己表現する「小悪魔」たち
(『小悪魔ageha メモリアルBook』)

　学校生活や社会に馴染むことのできない若者たちが、逸脱した行動をし、社会に対して抵抗する文化が「ヤンキー」です。

　例えば、ヤンキー文化は80年代の暴走族に現われていました。90年代以降は渋谷などで、「不良」少年少女たちが集団を形成し、抵抗的文化を作っていました。女子高生や女子大生の中で派手な化粧や髪を染める「ギャル」も、ヤンキーの文化を受け継いでいます。

　こうした集団は、仲間同士の関係を大切にしなが

AKB48

AKB48 is a "girl"(*shōjo*) idol group widely known for being "idols you can meet." They can be seen at a small theater in Akihabara every day. One of their activities is traveling around the country and shaking hands with their fans. Every year, about 300 candidates' ranking is decided based on votes from fans who purchased their CDs. AKB48 consists of about 100 members, divided into 6 "teams," with the top 7 members often appearing in the media. The top 16 are considered "selective members."

They practice, encourage, and compete with each other. Their fans support them in an almost parental fashion while watching their development. They can be objects of pseudo-romance to men, and of aspiration or empathy to women. Through dancing and songs performed by "regular girls," they convey the message that "one's best efforts will be repaid."

Yankee

"Yankee" in Japanese refers to a culture of resistance to society among youths who cannot adapt themselves to school life or mainstream society and pursue deviant behavior.

One of the best examples of this culture is motorcycle gangs in the 1980s. From the 1990s, "delinquent" boys and girls formed groups and created a culture of resistance. The female high-school and college students who wear flashy makeup or color their hair, so-called "*gyaru*" (gal), are successors to this Yankee culture.

Such groups share a feeling of resistance to society while valuing the ties with their comrades. They may be frowned upon by society but value discipline and pure spirit within their ranks. They emphasize practical things and taking action more

ら、社会への対抗精神を共有します。社会で顰蹙(ひんしゅく)を買うこともあるのですが、仲間同士で上下の規律や純粋な心も大切にしています。その中で知性を追求することよりも、実践と行動を起こすことを重んじます。覚悟を決め、気分を高め、中途半端なことはしないという精神です。何事にも気合を入れる感覚とも類似します。ヤンキーの精神は日本文化の底流を流れています。

【ファッション】

日本の若者のファッション感覚は多種多様です。世代ごとのスタイルに関するファッション雑誌が多数あり、同世代でも、雰囲気や感覚が異なります。

女性の場合、例えば、「OL」、「コンサバ」、「サーファー」、「ギャル」など異なるスタイルがあります。また、同じ人が、状況、会う相手、場所などに柔軟に対応し、異なるスタイルを形成し、多様な自己を演じます。同性の友達同士の平等な仲間意識を形成する手段でもあり、お互いに競い合います。美の基準は、センスが良いかどうか、「かわいい」かどうかです。異性よりは、同性からの承認を重視します。ファッションとは、何事にも前向きになろうとする意識を作る手段でもあります。

スマートフォンで自分を撮り、ネットに掲載していく女性たちも多くいます。承認の感覚を、実際の周囲の人たちだけでなく、ネット上で多数の人たちからも得ようとします。多様な場において、自分をファッションで演出しているのです。

（吉田光宏）

服を通じて楽しさを共有する
（『CanCam 2015年8月号』小学館）

than pursuing intelligence, and have a spirit of resolution, exuberance, and never doing anything halfway. This Yankee spirit, like firing oneself up for everything, is an undercurrent of Japanese culture.

Fashion

The fashion sense among Japanese youth has great variety. There are many fashion magazines for each generation, and the taste and style varies even among the same generation.

In the case of women, there are such styles as "office lady," "conservative," "surfer," and "gal." Moreover, one person may adopt different styles depending on the situation, place, and whom they meet, playing a multifaceted self. This is one of the ways in which people form a sense of fellowship with friends of the same gender, and they compete with each other. Their standard of beauty is whether something has good sense and is cute or not. They value recognition from others of the same gender more than from the opposite gender. Fashion is also a means of creating a consciousness of being positive towards everything.

Many women take selfies with their smartphones and post them on the Internet, seeking recognition from not only those around them but also many others online as well. They produce themselves through fashion in various scenes.

(Tr. A. T. Kamei-Dyche)

手塚治虫（ⓒ手塚プロダクション）

火の鳥（ⓒ手塚プロダクション）

【手塚治虫（1928-1989）】

　手塚治虫は「マンガの神」として知られる日本アニメの巨匠で、近代日本のマンガ・アニメ界を開拓・牽引した第一人者です。医学生として勉学に励む傍ら、プロの漫画家としての道を歩んだ人でした。

　手塚の登場によって、漫画の技術や構成はそれまでとは大きく変わりました。手塚漫画のキャラクターは、単純な線を用いながらも、心を揺さぶるような大きな目をもって描かれ、読者にとって感情移入しやすい存在でした。手塚はディズニーからの影響も受けていますが、ディズニーの現実逃避とは異なり、漫画を通して重大な問題提起やメッセージを人々に伝え、考えさせるきっかけをつくる作品を描きました。

　手塚の革新的な手法は日本のアニメをも変え、アニメーターの第一人者としてテレビアニメも制作しました。『鉄腕アトム』『ジャングル大帝』『ブラック・ジャック』『リボンの騎士』などが特に有名ですが、手塚自身が自分のライフワークとみなしていたのは『火の鳥』でした。

【スタジオジブリ】

　スタジオジブリは、長編アニメの制作を主とするアニメスタジオです。ジブリの前身はトップクラフトという会社で、宮﨑駿が『アニメージュ』に連載していた同名漫画をもとにつくられた『風の谷のナウシカ』（1984年）はトップクラフト時代の作品です。その後、徳間書店の助力を得て高畑勲と宮﨑が設立したのがジブリですが、この名称は第二次世界大戦期に使用されたイタリアの軍用機の名をとって命名されました。

Tezuka Osamu

Widely known as the "god of manga" as well as a major figure in the history of Japanese animation, Tezuka Osamu played a key role in the creation of Japan's modern manga and anime industries. Tezuka had a lifelong passion for drawing manga, and although he studied medicine as a student he took up the career of professional manga artist.

Tezuka had an enormous impact on manga, both technically and thematically. Seeking to draw the reader into the story, he made his manga dramatic by borrowing cinematic techniques. Simple characters with big evocative eyes were easy for readers to identify with. He was inspired by Disney, but contra Disney's escapism felt manga could prompt people to consider serious issues.

His innovations soon transformed Japanese animation as well, and he became a leading animator, pioneering television animation and not just feature films. Among his many works he is most well-known for *Mighty Atom* (Astro Boy), *Jungle Emperor* (Kimba the White Lion), *Black Jack*, and *Princess Knight*, although he felt his masterwork was *Phoenix*.

Studio Ghibli

Studio Ghibli is a major animation studio in Tokyo known for its feature-length films. Many Studio Ghibli works have become immensely popular and won numerous awards both in Japan and overseas.

Studio Ghibli had its origins in an older studio, Topcraft, that had achieved recognition for the hit film *Nausicaä of the Valley of the Wind* (1984), directed by Miyazaki Hayao based on a manga he had created for the magazine *Animage*. Later, Miyazaki and producer Takahata Isao, helped by Tokuma Shoten, started Studio Ghibli and carried over many Topcraft staff. Miyazaki named the studio after an Italian WWII-era

ジブリの初期の作品である『天空の城ラピュタ』(1986年)、『火垂るの墓』(1988年)、『となりのトトロ』(1988年) は、その完成度の高さと物語性の豊かさから高い評判を得、アニメの技術水準を上げる役割を果たしました。1997年の『もののけ姫』は大ヒットとなり、ジブリの名が世界的に知られるきっかけになりました。また、2001年に公開された『千と千尋の神隠し』は日本歴代興行収入の記録を塗りかえ、この記録は2020年まで破られていませんでした。

【オタク】

「オタク」とは、自分の好きなことに熱中しすぎる人のことです。「鉄道オタク」など、自分の好きなことに関してのみ膨大な知識をもつサブカルチャーグループも含まれますが、一般的にはアニメやマンガ、ゲームなどのファンを指します。

1980年代には「オタク」という言葉があまり良い意味では使われないことが多かったのですが、最近ではその傾向は弱まってきています。特に海外では、日本のポップカルチャーのファンであること以上の意味はありません。

アニメやマンガのオタクは、グッズの収集、コスプレをよくします。東京で年に2回開催されるコミケは世界最大規模の同人誌即売会で、毎回数十万人のファンが集まります。「オタクの街」として知られる東京・秋葉原はオタクの人気スポットです。

(亀井ダイチ・アンドリュー)

コミックマーケットカタログ88冊子版表紙
(コミックマーケット準備会)

airplane.

The studio's early films, *Laputa: Castle in the Sky* (1986), *Grave of the Fireflies* (1988), and *My Neighbor Totoro* (1988), cemented a reputation for touching but thought-provoking stories made to a high technical standard of animation. Ghibli first came to international prominence with *Princess Mononoke* (1997), a film that broke all previous box office records in Japan and stunned audiences with its rich and vibrant artwork. Another significant hit was *Spirited Away* (2001), which remained until 2020 the record-holder for Japanese box office earnings.

Otaku

"Otaku" is a Japanese word used for obsessive fans. While it can apply to anyone who is intensely dedicated to their hobby, it is most commonly used to refer to fans of anime, manga, and video games.

The term evolved in the 1980s and had mainly negative connotations; most serious fans were reluctant to use it to describe themselves. These days the word has less negative associations, especially overseas where it is used to just mean a fan of Japanese pop culture.

Anime and manga otaku like collecting items related to their favorite series (called "goods"), making fan fiction works (*dōjinshi*), and attending events like conventions where they dress up as characters. The Comic Market held twice a year in Tokyo is a major event attended by hundreds of thousands of fans. Akihabara is the area in Tokyo most associated with otaku culture and is now visited by fans from around the world.

(A. T. Kamei-Dyche)

海外におけるアニメと「クールジャパン」の誕生

　日本でアニメが作られるようになったのは大正時代ですが、日本のアニメの特徴である独特なキャラクターデザインと映画的な技法が生まれたのは、1960年代の手塚治虫の作品からでした。1970年代には多くのアニメシリーズが作られ、アメリカの子どもたちの間で人気を博しましたが、暴力やアルコール、宗教的な要素など子ども向けのアニメには不適切と思われるものは慎重に排除されました。キャラクターには西洋風な名前がつけられ、またタイトルも『科学忍者隊ガッチャマン』が*Battle of the Planets*、『宇宙戦艦ヤマト』は*Star Blazers*というふうに変えられました。

　1988年に映画化された『アキラ』は、国際的にも重要な成功を収め、SF映画の最高傑作の1つとして高い評価を得ました。1990年代半ばには『美少女戦士セーラームーン』や『ドラゴンボールZ』といったテレビ番組が海外で大人気となり、また『ポケットモンスター』の成功は、アニメやゲームなどが大きな利益をもたらすことを多くの国々で証明する結果となりました。

　海外ではファンが独自に母語の字幕を付けたり、二次創作をしたり、コンベンションを開催したりしました。2000年までに「アニメ」は一般的な英語になっています。アニメの内容は編集されることが多いのですが、以前と違ってあまり「欧米化」はされず、主題歌や挿入歌は日本語の曲がそのまま使われる場合もありました。

　日本政府は当初アニメ人気を過小評価しており、海外でのアニメの普及に対してあまり熱心ではありませんでした。アニメが膨大な消費を産み、経済的利益をもたらす可能性に気付くと、日本政府は日本のポップカルチャーを海外に発信するための「クールジャパン」政策を推進し始めます。日本のアニメは世界中で高い評価を受け続けており、現在では最も有名な日本文化の1つとなっています。

　　　　　　　　　　　　　　　　（亀井ダイチ・アンドリュー）

Anime Overseas and the Birth of "Cool Japan"

Japanese animation dates from the Taishō period, but Japanese animation only began to develop most of its defining character designs and cinematographic techniques with the work of Tezuka Osamu in the early 1960s. During the 1970s there were many more series produced, and anime was popular among American children, but shows were carefully edited to remove content deemed inappropriate such as overt violence, alcohol, and religious references. Characters were often given Western names, and series were renamed: *Kagaku Ninjatai Gatchaman* became *Battle of the Planets*, while *Uchū Senkan Yamato* became *Star Blazers*.

The film *Akira* (1988) was an international success, and was recognized as one of the best science fiction films. In the mid-1990s, the TV shows *Sailor Moon* and *Dragon Ball Z* became overseas sensations. The success of *Pocket Monsters* in many countries proved that anime and games could be enormously profitable.

Overseas fans subtitled anime in their own languages, produced derivative works, and held conventions. By the year 2000, "anime" had become a household word in English. While often still edited for content, anime series were less "Westernized," and some even retained the original Japanese-language theme songs.

Initially, the Japanese government underestimated the popularity of anime and was unenthusiastic about its spread overseas. The government gradually came to recognize the financial opportunity anime represented, and launched the "Cool Japan" initiative to market Japanese pop culture overseas. Japanese animation continues to be enjoyed around the world, and is now one of Japan's most famous cultural products. (Tr. A. T. Kamei-Dyche)

❖日本の世界文化遺産❖

⓫ 石見銀山遺跡とその文化的景観
Iwami Ginzan Silver Mine and its Cultural Landscape

《世界に知られた銀の産地》

　石見銀山は、16世紀から20世紀の銀の採掘・精錬施設などを中心とした銀の鉱山地帯です。この銀鉱は、日本の金銀の生産を促進し、また東南アジア全体の経済発展に貢献しました。銀鉱山跡と鉱山町、港と港町、及びこれらをつなぐ街道が遺産地域に含まれており、鉱山開発や土地利用の総体を表わす文化的景観の価値が認められています。

【所在地】島根県　【登録年】2007年
【写　真】龍源寺間歩（提供：大田市教育委員会）

12

西洋との出会い

Encountering the West

【出島】

出島とは、江戸時代の初期、1636年にキリスト教の布教を禁止し、長崎市内に雑居していたポルトガル人を収容するために、幕府によって長崎港に作られた面積1万3000m²の埋立地です。

1639年、ポルトガル人は出島から追放され、1641年に平戸からオランダ商館が移転されると、それ以降はオランダと中国の商人のみが出島で貿易を許されました。

その後、1858年の安政5か国条約によって、日本が通商を始めるために開国するまでの約220年間、出島は西欧に開かれた唯一の窓として、日本の近代化に重要な役割を果たしました。なお、来航したオランダ船は、1621年から1847年までに延べ700隻以上に上りました。

船が入港すると、阿蘭陀(オランダ)通詞は商館長を訪れ、情報を聞き取って翻訳し、それを長崎奉行が江戸に送りました。この文書は「風説書」と呼ばれ、幕府が海外情勢を知る最も重要な情報源となりました。

出島図（長崎歴史文化博物館収蔵）

【洋学】

江戸時代後期を中心にして、西欧の語学の研究、外国語の修得を通して学ばれた自然科学・社会科学・人文科学など、西洋の学術研究の総称が洋学です。

鎖国政策により、西洋の学術・文化は、唯一である長崎の出島を経由して、オランダ語を媒介として日本にもたらされました。これは蘭学と呼ばれ、青木昆陽・杉田玄白・前野良沢・大槻玄沢ら多数の蘭学者が輩出し、医学・数学・天文学・暦学などの諸分

杉田玄白 80歳の頃の肖像画（重要文化財：早稲田大学図書館所蔵）

Dejima

In 1636, at the beginning of the Edo period, the Tokugawa bakufu prohibited Christian missionary activities, and built the artificial island of Dejima in Nagasaki harbor, covering an area of 13,000 m², to accommodate all the Portuguese who were living in the city at the time.

In 1639, the Portuguese were expelled from Dejima. In 1641, the employees of the Dutch East India Company Trading Post were transferred to Dejima from Hirado, and after that only Dutch and Chinese traders were allowed to do business on the island.

For 220 years, until 1858, when Japan opened for foreign trade under the *Ansei* Five-Power Treaties, Dejima was the only window open on to the West and as such played a very important role in Japan's modernization. From 1621 to 1847, more than 700 Dutch ships docked in Dejima.

Whenever a ship docked, the Japanese interpreter visited the Dutch officials to gather information, which the Nagasaki magistrate then conveyed to the bakufu in Edo. The documents containing that information were called *fūsetsu-gaki* and they were an extremely valuable means for the bakufu to learn about the situation overseas.

Western Learning

"Western learning" is the generic term used particularly in the late Edo period to refer to the body of knowledge which was developed in Japan through the study and learning of foreign languages, and which included Western disciplines such as the natural, social, and human sciences.

Because of the *sakoku* ("locked country") policy, the science and culture of the West entered Japan — through the Dutch language — solely via the island of Dejima in Nagasaki. This body of knowledge was called *rangaku* ("Dutch learning") and it developed across a variety of disciplines such as medicine, mathematics, astronomy, or the study of calendars. Famous

野にわたり発展しました。

19世紀後半、幕末に至って通商条約が締結され、日本は鎖国から開国に大きく舵を切ったことから、オランダ人以外の外国人も多数来日しました。それに伴い、イギリス・フランスなどの学術・文化が、それぞれの国の言語とともにもたらされました。

洋学という言葉は、これ以降定着し、英学が蘭学にかわって主要な地位を占めることになりました。また、洋学は、西洋の知識・技術を移入する際にも力を発揮し、明治国家の建設の礎になりました。

【留学生】

欧米列強によって、開国を余儀なくされた幕末の日本は、植民地化を回避するために、西洋の文明、特に海軍を中心とする軍事技術を習得する必要に迫られました。

そのため、海を渡った日本人が多数いました。大別すると、幕府から派遣された遣欧米使節団と留学生です。留学先としては、イギリスが最も多く、次いで、アメリカ、オランダでした。

留学生の多くは、国禁を犯した諸藩からの派遣であり、総数では130人に上りました。中でも、特に有名なのは、富国強兵に役立つ有為な人材となる使命を帯びた長州ファイブや薩摩スチューデントといった、主として西国雄藩からの密航留学生でした。

外国を見聞した留学生、例えば伊藤博文などが帰国後にもたらした経験や知識によって、その後の日本が形作られたこと、つまり彼らが明治近代国家の礎になったことは重要な事実です。　　　　（町田明広）

長州ファイブ（萩博物館所蔵）

薩摩スチューデント
（鹿児島県立図書館所蔵）

rangaku scholars include Aoki Kon'yō, Sugita Genpaku, Maeno Ryōtaku, and Ōtsuki Gentaku.

In the second half of the 19th century, with the end of the bakufu government and the signing of the trade treaties, when Japan steered away from the *sakoku* policy to become an open country, numerous foreigners other than the Dutch started coming to Japan. Thus, science and culture from England, France and other countries entered Japan along with their respective languages.

The term "Western learning" established itself around this time, as "English learning" came to supersede "Dutch learning." "Western learning" was highly influential in the introduction of knowledge and technology from the West, and became one of the pillars on which the Meiji state was built.

Studying Abroad

Japan, which had to open in the final years of the Edo period under pressure from the Western powers, was forced to acquire staples of Western civilization such as know-how in military technology — particularly naval technology — in order to avoid colonization.

As a result, there were a lot of Japanese people who went abroad. They fell into two big categories: those in the official missions the bakufu dispatched to Europe and the United States, and those who went to study abroad. Most of the students went to England, followed by the United States and Holland.

Many of the 130 students were sent abroad by the *han* ("provinces") that disobeyed the official policy. The most famous among them were the "Chōshū Five" and the "Satsuma Students," stowaways from the rich provinces in Western Japan who would later on assume the mission of being key persons in implementing the Meiji objective of *fukoku kyōhei* ("enrich the country, strengthen the military").

It was the experience and knowledge that these students — like Itō Hirobumi — who caught a glimpse of foreign countries brought back that became the foundations of the Meiji modern state and shaped Japan in the following years.   (Tr. R. Paşca)

【切支丹】

　キリスト教の日本への伝来は、戦国時代の最中の1549年で、カトリックの一派であるイエズス会のフランシスコ・ザビエル司祭（1506-1552）による布教だとされています。「切支丹」（キリシタン）とは、ポルトガル語から来ている外来語であり、もともとの意味は「キリスト教徒」です。日本では、戦国時代から明治時代のはじめごろにかけて、カトリックの信者や伝道者を指すために使われていた言葉です。

　伝来から半世紀ほど経ち信者の数が7万人を越えたと言われている1614年に、徳川家康の禁教令によってキリスト教は禁止され、キリシタンの取り締まりが始まりました。

　そのような中で信仰を捨てずに密かに祈禱書を唱えたり祈りを続けたりした信者は「隠れキリシタン」、または「潜伏キリシタン」と呼ばれていました。特に幕府から比較的遠い長崎県や熊本県などで、明治のキリスト教解禁まで「隠れキリシタン」の多くの組織が存続していました。

「聖フランシスコ・ザヴィエル像」（神戸市立博物館所蔵　Photo: Kobe City Museum/DNPartcom）

【宣教師】

　戦国時代から江戸時代にかけてポルトガルなどの国から数多くのキリスト教徒が日本にやってきました。当時、「切支丹」と呼ばれていましたが、その中で一番有名な人物は1549年に鹿児島に上陸したフランシスコ・ザビエルというカトリック教会の司祭です。ザビエルに続き、多くのイエズス会員が日本を訪れますが、彼らによる活動の方針は現地の文化を尊重しながらキリスト教の教えを広めることでした。

Christians

The spread of Christianity in Japan is considered to have started in 1549 during the Sengoku period with the missionary work of Francis Xavier (1506-1552), a Jesuit monk. The word *kirishitan*, which comes from the Portuguese *cristão*, actually means "Christian", and it was used in Japan from the Sengoku period until the beginning of the Meiji period to refer to believers and missionaries of the Catholic faith.

In 1614, about half a century after the advent of Christianity, when the number of Christians is said to have reached more than 70,000, the religion was banned by an official act of the shogun Tokugawa Ieyasu, which marked the beginning of regulatory actions against the Christians.

The believers who did not renounce their faith and still continued to read religious books and pray were called "hidden Christians" (*kakure*, or *senpuku kirishitan*). Many communities of "hidden Christians" remained active until the final years of the Edo period, especially in areas further from the bakufu like Nagasaki or Kumamoto.

Missionaries

From the Sengoku period through the Edo period, many Christian missionaries came to Japan from Portugal and other countries. They were called *kirishitan* in Japanese. The most famous of them is Francis Xavier, a Catholic monk who arrived in Kagoshima in 1549. After him, numerous other Jesuits visited Japan with the mission of spreading Christianity while respecting the local culture.

Under guidance from these missionaries, many Japanese people became Christians in a short period of time and among them were even some local lords (*daimyō*) who converted, like

高山右近像
（写真提供：高槻市）

これらの宣教師の活動により短期間で多くの日本人がキリスト教徒になりましたが、その中には高山右近、大友義鎮（宗麟）、大村純忠などの「キリシタン大名」もいました。

宣教師たちは初めて日本にリキュールや鉄砲を持ち込んだという説もあります。さらに、「パン」や「てんぷら」など、現代日本語でも使われているいくつかの単語も、ポルトガル人の宣教師の影響によるものだと言われています。

【『日本大文典』】

『日本大文典』（国際日本文化研究センター所蔵）

キリスト教の布教が目的で渡ってきたキリシタンたちが宣教師として活躍しましたが、早い段階から現地の言語、つまり、日本語を習得する必要性に迫られました。

そのような中で、イエズス会のジョアン・ロドリゲスというポルトガル人の宣教師が、1604年から08年にかけて *Arte da Lingoa de Iapam*（『日本大文典』）というタイトルで初の日本語学書を長崎で刊行しました。この書は、当時の口語文法を中心に日本語をラテン語学の枠組みに基づいて体系的に説明したもので、ポルトガル語によって詳細に記述しています。

この『日本大文典』は、1603年に刊行された日本語ポルトガル語対訳辞書 *Vocabulário da Língua do Japão*（『日葡辞書』）とともに宣教師による教育実践の活動でよく使用されるようになり、これが日本における日本語教育の始まりだと言われています。

（ロマン・パシュカ）

『日葡辞書』（国際日本文化研究センター所蔵）

Takayama Ukon, Ōtomo Yoshishige or Ōmura Sumitada. They were called "Christian daimyō."

Missionaries are said to have introduced liqueur and firearms to Japan. Also, "pan," "tempura" and a few other words which are still in use in contemporary Japanese are considered to be an influence of the presence of the Portuguese missionaries.

Japanese Grammar Book

The Christians who came to Japan with the purpose of spreading Christianity were very active as missionaries, and from an early stage they felt the need to learn Japanese, the language of the locals.

It was in this context that the Portuguese missionary João Rodrigues, a member of the Society of Jesus, published in Nagasaki between 1604 and 1608 the first Japanese language grammar book titled *Arte da Lingoa de Iapam* (*Nihon daibunten*). The book gives a systematic description of the Japanese language spoken at the time using the framework of Latin grammar, with detailed explanations in Portuguese.

Together with the Japanese-Portuguese dictionary *Vocabulário da Língua do Japão* (*Nippo jisho*) published in 1603, this grammar book was often used by the missionaries in their teaching practice. This is considered to represent the beginning of Japanese language teaching in Japan. (R. Paşca)

明治維新から150年
～近代日本のスタートを知る～

　2018年は明治維新から150年目の節目にあたります。それを記念して、鹿児島県や山口県など各地で観光イベントなど、様々な事業が行われました。

　幕末は、江戸時代（1603-1867）の終焉直前、1853年のアメリカ使節ペリーの来航から始まったとされます。それまでの日本は、鎖国を対外方針としていたため、ペリーは和親と通商、つまり開国を求めに来たのです。幕府は、巧みに通商を回避して和親条約を結んだものの、1858年、日米修好通商条約が結ばれました。

　これによって、帝国主義によるアジア侵略や自由貿易主義に巻き込まれることになりました。最大の難問は早く近代化を果たし、列強の侵略を跳ね返すほどの国力を整え、植民地になる危険を回避することでした。

　しかし、勅許がない通商条約の即時破棄を主張する長州藩や過激な廷臣は、幕府に攘夷実行を迫って対立を深めました。過激な攘夷行動を嫌う孝明天皇は、会津藩や薩摩藩と連携し、長州藩勢力を京都から完全に追放しました。

　欧米列強の圧力により、1865年に通商条約は勅許され、対外方針をめぐる政争は終止符を打ちました。その後は植民地化を回避できる政体をどのようにするかにありました。つまり、幕府を強化するのか、王政復古を目指すかにあり、それは幕府対薩摩藩・長州藩の構図となりました。

　長州征伐に失敗した幕府は、一層権威を失墜し、1867年に至り、将軍慶喜は大政奉還を行い、さらには1869年の戊辰戦争の敗北によって、完全に瓦解しました。幕藩体制という封建制の崩壊を踏まえ、明治新政府は近代的立憲国家の建設に向けて、スタートを切りました。

（町田明広）

150 Years since the Meiji Restoration
Learning about the Beginnings of Modern Japan

2018 marks the 150-year commemoration of the Meiji Restoration in Japan. To celebrate this, various projects or tourist events were held in Kagoshima, Yamaguchi, and other parts of Japan.

Bakumatsu refers to the final years of the Edo period (1603-1867) and is considered to have begun in 1853 with the arrival of Commodore Perry's fleet. Until then, Japan's position toward foreign countries had been one of isolation (*sakoku*), but Perry demanded that Japan open up to foreign trade. At first, the bakufu managed to avoid establishing trade and only signed a Convention of Peace and Amity. However, in 1858, the Treaty of Amity and Commerce was signed between Japan and the U.S..

As a result, Japan became involved in free trade and the colonization of Asia, motivated by imperialism. Its most difficult task was to modernize as fast as possible, and to strengthen its position so as to be able to repel any invasion in order to avoid colonization.

However, the Chōshū domain and the radical court officials, who demanded cancellation of the treaty because it had not been sanctioned by the emperor, destabilized the political situation by demanding that the bakufu expel foreigners. Emperor Kōmei, who disliked the idea of a radical exclusion of foreigners, cooperated with the Aizu and Satsuma domains and banished Chōshū leaders out of Kyoto.

Because of the pressure from Western powers, the commercial treaty was sanctioned in 1865, and the turmoil surrounding the policy toward foreigners came to an end. It was a question of whether to strengthen the bakufu, or to attempt a restoration of Imperial rule. The bakufu on the one hand, and the Satsuma and Chōshū domains on the other had antagonistic positions in this respect.

The authority of the bakufu weakened after the failure of the Chōshū expeditions. In 1867, shogun Yoshinobu achieved the restoration of imperial rule and, after the defeat in the Boshin War of 1869, the bakufu collapsed completely. After the collapse of the shogunate, the new Meiji government started to build a modern constitutional state.

(Tr. R. Paşca)

❖日本の世界文化遺産❖

平泉 〜仏国土（浄土）を表す建築・庭園及び考古学的遺跡群〜
Hiraizumi 〜 Temples, Gardens and Archaeological Sites Representing the Buddhist Pure Land 〜

《平安を願って表現された奥州藤原氏の建築・庭園》

◉

　浄土を表わす寺院、庭園及び考古学的遺跡から成るこの遺産は、聖なる山である金鶏山を含む５つの資産で構成されています。平泉は、11世紀から12世紀に京都と肩を並べる日本の北方領域の政治・行政上の拠点でした。その空間は、８世紀に日本に広まった浄土の世界観に基づいており、人々が来世とともに現世の平安を切望して仏国土（浄土）を表現したものです。

◉

【所在地】岩手県　【登録年】2011年
【写　真】毛越寺浄土庭園大泉が池（提供：毛越寺）

近代教育の始まり
The Beginning of Modern Education

【学校制度】

　日本の現在の学校制度は、教育レベル別に修業年限区分を設ける６・３・３制（小学校６年、中学校３年、高等学校３年）をとっています。高等学校は義務教育ではありませんが、中卒での就職が困難なため、ほとんど必須とみなされています。公立の他、多様な私立校があります。高等教育レベルでは、大学（２年制の短期大学、４年制の学部教育および大学院を含む）、また高等専門学校や様々な専修学校があります。公立での義務教育以外、ほとんどの学校では入学試験が課されるため、多くの生徒が希望する進学先に進むために塾に通います。

　日本では学歴の高い人が多い傾向があり、海外においても比較的高い評価を得ています。しかし、その一方で日本の教育機関は暗記学習や受験対策に重点を置き過ぎ、批判的な分析能力を養う教育をしていないという批判も浴びています。また、高等教育以前では、生徒間によるいじめも、大きな社会問題になっています。

【お雇い外国人】

　お雇い外国人とは、幕末から明治時代にかけて、技術や産業、学術など各分野の欧米の先進文化を日本に移入するために、日本が雇った外国人のことをいいます。実学の指導のほか、諸外国の文化や社会事情を伝えるために雇用された外国人もおり、彼らは日本の近代化にとても重要な役割を果たしました。日本政府が公式に雇用した人もいれば、民間で雇用された人もいます。実際の総人数は正確には分かって

Educational System

The contemporary Japanese education system incorporates a 6-3-3 model (6 years of elementary school, 3 years of junior high school, and 3 years of high school). While high school is technically not compulsory, due to the difficulty of finding employment for junior high school graduates it is all but mandatory. There is a broad range of both public and private high schools. At the post-secondary level there are also short-term and regular university programs, and numerous professional schools. A large part of education consists of studying for the entrance examinations at each level of the system. Many students attend cram schools (*juku*) after class to help prepare themselves.

Generally, Japanese students have a high literacy rate and a high rate of educational advancement. They also score highly on international assessments. On the other hand, Japanese schools face criticism for their emphasis on rote learning and teaching test preparation rather than critical skills. Moreover, students may face serious social issues like bullying.

Hired Foreigners

In the Bakumatsu and Meiji eras, the Japanese government recruited foreigners to instruct Japanese in the newest technology, industry, and fields of knowledge. As such, they played a key role in the early stages of Japanese modernization. Along with practical and scientific knowledge, some foreigners were hired to provide information about foreign cultures and societies. Along with the many official hires, there were also foreigners hired by the private sector. The total number of these individuals is unknown but it was certainly many thousands.

Some of these hired foreigners later became international experts on aspects of Japanese culture and history who

いませんが、数千人に上ったとみられています。

お雇い外国人の中から、後に日本の歴史や文化の専門家として、日本を西洋に紹介する人々が誕生しました。海外の日本研究の先駆者の1人であるバジル・ホール・チェンバレン（英）や、作家として名高いラフカディオ・ハーン（ギリシャ／日本名・小泉八雲）、美術研究家のアーネスト・フェノロサ（米）、著述家のウィリアム・グリフィス（米）、技師のウィリアム・K・バートン（英）らが有名です。

【寺子屋】

寺子屋とは、江戸時代に町人の子弟らに読み書きを教えた民間の教育施設です。当初は寺院で行われていたことから、その名がついています。寺子屋は江戸中期における商人層の増加によって激増し、大都市のみならず地方の小都市や農村・漁村を含め全国に広く普及しました。一方、武士の子弟は寺子屋ではなく、儒学者を師として藩校などで学びました。

幕末期には、江戸に住む庶民の大半が寺子屋で学んだ経験がありました。師となったのは僧や武士、また教育を受けた町人出身者などです。寺子屋は通常、師匠の自宅で開かれており、読み書き算盤などの基礎的な実務教育だけではなく、古典や音楽を教える師匠もいました。

寺子と呼ばれる生徒たちは午前と午後に寺子屋に通い、各自のペースで勉強をすすめました。幕末期における町方人口の識字率は世界最高水準に達していますが、これは寺子屋の果たした役割が大きかったためと高く評価されています。

（亀井ダイチ・アンドリュー）

「稚六芸ノ内　書数」
歌川国定
（都立中央図書館特別文庫室所蔵）

「文学万代の宝　始の巻」一寸子花里画
（都立中央図書館特別文庫室所蔵）

introduced Japan to the Western world. These included scholar and pioneering Japanologist Basil Hall Chamberlain (UK), writer Lafcadio Hearn (Greece; he took the Japanese name Koizumi Yakumo), art expert Ernest Fenollosa (USA), author William Elliot Griffis (USA), and engineer William Kinnimond Burton (UK).

Temple Schools

Temple schools (*terakoya*) were private institutions that taught commoner children reading and writing during the Edo period. They originally developed from schools operated on the grounds of Buddhist temples, hence the name. They grew in number dramatically from the middle of the Edo period when the merchant class in large cities expanded. However, they also existed in smaller towns and even rural areas. The children of samurai, meanwhile, usually attended elite academies headed by leading scholars.

By the end of the Edo period, the majority of commoners in the capital, Edo, had experience attending a temple school. Each school usually had just one teacher, often a monk, samurai, or educated commoner, with classes being held at the teacher's residence. In addition to reading and writing, instructors taught arithmetic, and some even classical literature or traditional music.

Students normally attended in the morning and afternoon, and progressed at their own pace. Temple schools have been credited with the reasonably high literacy rate of Japanese townspeople at the end of the Edo period. (A. T. Kamei-Dyche)

13│近代教育の始まり

【シーボルト (1796-1866)】

キヨソネ筆シーボルト
肖像（シーボルト記念
館所蔵）

　ドイツ人医師・博物学者。1823年、オランダ商館付医員として、長崎の出島に到着しました。日本人を診療し、また鳴滝塾を開き、全国から集う塾生に医学などを教えました。ここで学んだ人々は、やがて医者や学者として、全国で幅広く活躍しました。

　1826年、シーボルトはオランダ商館長の江戸参府に同行し、将軍に謁見したり、多くの医者や学者に会ってお互いの知識や情報を交換したり、日本研究に役立てるための品物を譲り受けたりしました。

　江戸参府の後、「シーボルト事件」が起こりました。シーボルトが日本調査のため集めた品物の中に、日本から持ち出すことが禁じられていた日本地図があったため、1829年に国外追放の処分を受けました。

　オランダに帰ったシーボルトは、日本で集めた資料や知識をもとにして、日本についての本格的な研究書である『日本』や、日本の植物・動物を紹介する『日本植物誌』『日本動物誌』などを出版し、西洋における日本学の発展に大きく貢献しました。

シーボルト書簡
（神田外語大学附属図
書館所蔵）

【ヘボン (1815-1911)】

ヘボン肖像
（資料提供：明治学院
歴史資料館）

　アメリカ人宣教師・医師。開業医としてニューヨークで大成功を収めていましたが、全財産をなげうって、幕末激動の日本に渡航する決心を固め、1859年に来日しました。横浜に居を構え、西洋医術を日本人に施しながら、聖書の翻訳を目指して日本語研究に着手しました。

　ヘボンは、1863年にヘボン塾を開き、明治期以降の国家リーダーとなる高橋是清・林董・益田孝など

Philipp Franz Balthasar von Siebold

Siebold was a German physician and botanist. In 1823 he arrived at Dejima (a small artificial island serving as a Dutch trading post) in Nagasaki as a doctor for a Dutch trading house. He treated Japanese patients, and established Narutaki-Juku to teach medical science and the like to students who came from all over Japan. These students went on to play active roles all over the country as doctors or scholars.

In 1826, Siebold accompanied the curator of the Dutch trading house on a visit to Edo, where he was able to see the Shogun, and exchange knowledge and information with many other doctors and scholars, as well as receive items useful for his studies of Japan.

It was after the visit to Edo when the "Siebold Incident" occurred. Among the items he had collected for his research on Japan were maps of the country, the export of which was strictly prohibited. As a result, Siebold was banished from Japan in 1829.

After returning to the Netherlands, he published several books on Japan, including a full-scale study of the country (*Nippon*), and studies of Japanese plants and animals (*Flora Japonica* and *Fauna Japonica*), through which he remarkably contributed to the development of Japan studies in the West.

James Curtis Hepburn

Hepburn was an American physician and lay Christian missionary. Despite having success as a medical practitioner in New York, he decided to come to Japan in 1859, during the turmoil at the end of the Tokugawa era, at the cost of all of his property. He settled in Yokohama and started researching the Japanese language with the aim of translating the Bible, while providing Western medical treatment to Japanese.

He established a private school in 1863 and taught English to several notable leaders-to-be of the Meiji period onwards, such as Takahashi Korekiyo, Hayashi Tadasu, Masuda Takashi. The school later developed into Meiji Gakuin University and Ferris

『和英語林集成』〈初版〉和文扉
（神田外語大学附属図書館所蔵）

に英語教育を行いました。塾はその後、明治学院・フェリス女学院に発展し、ヘボン自身は1889年に、明治学院初代総理となりました。

また、1867年、ローマ字表記の『和英語林集成』を出版しました。これに用いたローマ字は、後にヘボン式ローマ字として普及し、現在に至ります。

ヘボンは1880年に新約聖書、1888年には旧約聖書の文語体訳を完成し、念願を叶えました。こうした活動を通じて、ヘボンは日本におけるプロテスタントの伝道と教育の基礎を築いたと言えます。

【アーネスト・サトウ（1843-1929）】

アーネスト・サトウ

イギリス人外交官。1862年、生麦事件の発生直前に横浜に到着しました。そして、1863年に薩英戦争に従軍し、1864年には四国連合艦隊下関砲撃事件で、講和会議の通訳を勤めました。

サトウは1865年に日本語通訳官、1868年には書記官に昇任、歴代のイギリス公使の下で、維新の激動期における日英外交に従事しました。また、西郷隆盛、坂本龍馬ら多数の志士との意見交換を試み、幕末政局の動向について、情報収集に努めました。

1866年には、『ジャパン・タイムス紙』に対日外交問題についての論説を発表、『英国策論』という訳本で広く読まれ、政局に大きな影響を与えました。1895年には、駐日特命全権公使に就任しています。

サトウには、『英日国語辞書』『中部・北部日本旅行案内』など、日本語および日本事情研究の著書も多く、イギリスにおける日本学の基礎の確立に寄与しました。彼の日記は、幕末維新史の一級資料として、現在も幅広く活用されています。　　　　（町田明広）

『改正増補英和対訳袖珍辞書』アーネスト・サトウ蔵書票
（神田外語大学附属図書館所蔵）

University. Hepburn himself became the first president of Meiji Gakuin University in 1889.

He also published *Japanese-English Dictionary; with an English and Japanese Index*, which rendered Japanese in the Latin alphabet (*romaji*), in 1867. Hepburn's system of rendering Japanese, "Hepburn romanization," spread and is still in use today.

He completed literary-style translations of the New Testament in 1880 and the Old Testament in 1888, achieving his dearest wish. Through such activities, he established a foundation for Protestant preaching and education in Japan.

Sir Ernest Mason Satow

Sir Ernest Satow was a British diplomat. He arrived in Yokohama in 1862, just before the outbreak of the Namamugi Incident (when a British national was killed by samurai retainers). He participated in the Anglo-Satsuma War in 1863, and served as an interpreter at the peace conference following the bombardment of Shimonoseki by four Western countries in 1864.

Satow worked as a Japanese interpreter in 1865 and was promoted to secretary in 1868, continuing to be involved in Anglo-Japanese diplomacy under a succession of British ministers during the tempestuous Restoration period. He also sought to exchange ideas with political activists like Saigō Takamori and Sakamoto Ryōma, and gather information concerning the political situation of the time.

In 1866, Satow published some articles concerning diplomacy with Japan in the *Japan Times*. The Japanese translations, entitled *Eikoku Sakuron*, were widely read and had an enormous impact on contemporary Japanese politics.

Satow also wrote many books about Japanese language, culture, and society, such as an *English-Japanese Dictionary*, and *A Handbook for Travellers in Central and Northern Japan*. He established the foundation of Japan Studies in Britain. Further, his diary is an essential historical source for the Bakumatsu-Restoration era, and is widely studied today.

(Tr. A. T. Kamei-Dyche)

江戸時代の外国との交流

　江戸時代（1603-1867）の日本を支配していた徳川幕府は、東アジアを事実上支配する中国帝国の国際体制である「冊封(さくほう)」の外に日本を位置付け、海禁の一形態ともいえる「鎖国」政策を採用しました。鎖国とは、日本人の海外渡航・帰国を厳禁し、外国船は追い払うことを骨子としており、キリスト教を徹底的に排除しました。

　日本は、17世紀前半から約250年間「鎖国」をしていましたが、完全に世界から孤立していたわけではありません。幕府は、外に向かって開かれた4つの口(くち)を持っていました。アイヌとは松前藩経由、オランダ・中国とは長崎（出島）、朝鮮とは対馬藩経由、琉球とは薩摩藩経由で交易を行いながら、世界情報を入手しました。

　中でも、出島に来たオランダ人によって、最先端の西洋文明が多方面にわたってもたらされ、蘭学として日本の知識人に浸透しました。特に語学・医学・天文学・物理学・測量学・化学といった分野の発展は著しく、日本の近代化に大きく貢献することになりました。

　1853年、アメリカ使節ペリーが浦賀に来航し、日本に開国を迫り、日米和親条約が締結されました。次いで1858年、日米修好通商条約が結ばれ、貿易が始まって外国人が国内に居留を始め、文字通り、日本は開国することになりました。こうして約250年続いた鎖国は終止符を打ち、日本は国際社会の一員となったのです。

　開国によって、それまでの蘭学に加え、英語による英学などの新たな西洋の学問が流入を始め、これらを総称する洋学へと発展し、中でも軍事技術の導入に大きな貢献を果たしました。

　開国を契機に、日本は幕末という動乱期に突入し、ペリー来航後、わずか15年で明治維新を成し遂げました。近世から近代の幕開けにあたり、明治国家の発展に西洋文明は大きく寄与しました。

（町田明広）

13 | The Beginning of Modern Education

Foreign Relations During the Edo Period

During the Edo period (1603-1867), the Tokugawa Bakufu decided to situate Japan outside the Chinese tributary system and pursued a seclusion policy by banning maritime activities. Emphasis was placed on banning travel by Japanese to and from the country, driving away foreign ships, and the total elimination of Christianity.

From the early 17th century Japan was in seclusion for nearly 250 years, but it was not totally isolated from the rest of the world. The Bakufu kept four windows open to the outside. There was trade with the Ainu through Matsumae domain, with the Netherlands and China through Dejima in Nagasaki, with Choson Korea through Tsushima domain, and with the Ryūkyūs through Satsuma domain. Through these trade relations, the Bakufu was able to obtain information about world affairs.

Many cultural developments and technologies from the West were brought by the Dutch coming to Dejima, and were studied by Japanese intellectuals under the name *rangaku* (Dutch learning). Languages, medical science, astronomy, physics, land surveying and chemistry were particularly important, and contributed significantly to Japan's modernization.

In 1853, Commodore Perry arrived at Uraga to demand Japan open its doors. The Treaty of Peace and Amity between the United States and Japan was concluded in the following year. In 1858, the Treaty of Amity and Commerce was also concluded with the US, trading began, and foreigners started to live within Japan. With this opening of the country, the seclusion of nearly 250 years ended, and Japan joined international society.

Many new fields of study, such as British studies carried out in English, were introduced on top of the preexisting Dutch studies, leading to "Western learning." This made a great contribution, particularly to the introduction of military technology.

Following the opening of the country, Japan entered an unsteady time known as bakumatsu. Only 15 years after Perry's arrival, the Meiji Restoration occurred. Japan transformed from an early modern state to a modern one, a process in which Western civilization played a major role. (Tr. A. T. Kamei-Dyche)

❖日本の世界文化遺産❖

富士山〜信仰の対象と芸術の源泉〜
Fujisan 〜 Sacred Place and Source of Artistic Inspiration 〜

《日本人の心のよりどころであり続ける名峰》

　富士山は標高3776mの成層火山。その威厳のある山容と断続的な噴火は宗教的な霊感を人々に抱かせ、古くから死と蘇りを象徴する登拝が行われてきました。山頂には浅間大神が住むと信じられ、山裾に浅間神社や御師の家が形成されました。また、富士山の美しい姿を表現した葛飾北斎の『富嶽三十六景』は、富士山を世界中に知らしめるとともに、西洋絵画の発展に大きな影響を与えました。

【所在地】山梨県・静岡県　【登録年】2013年
【写　真】富士山（提供：やまなし観光推進機構）

14 近現代の歩み

The Course of Modernity

【日清戦争／日露戦争】

《日清戦争》
平壌の戦いを描いた錦絵（国立国会図書館デジタルコレクション）

日本が開国した19世紀後半、経済力・軍事力に優る欧米列強が、アジア、アフリカなどで植民地を拡大していました。明治日本の指導者は、朝鮮半島が外国の支配下に入ると、日本の安全が脅かされると考えていました。朝鮮の支配権をめぐって、清（中国）と戦ったのが日清戦争（1894-1895）、ロシアと戦ったのが日露戦争（1904-1905）です。2つの戦争に勝利した日本は、1910年に大韓帝国を併合し、植民地としました。中国大陸でも権益を手に入れます。

日露戦争の日本の勝利は、アジアの国が欧米の強国を破ったものとして、アジア諸民族のナショナリズムを刺激しました。イギリスの植民地であったインドの独立運動家ネルーも、日本の勝利がアジアの人々に喜びをもって迎えられたと述べています。しかし、その後の日本の行動については「少数の侵略的帝国主義諸国のグループに、もう1国をつけ加えたというにすぎなかった」と批判しています。

《日露戦争》
連合艦隊司令長官・東郷平八郎の銅像と戦艦三笠
（写真提供：横須賀市）

【第一次世界大戦】

1914年ドイツを中心とする国々とイギリスを中心とする国々との間で、戦争が始まりました。第一次世界大戦（1914-1918）です。日本も日英同盟に基づいて参戦します。ただし、主戦場である欧州から遠く離れていたため、小規模な戦闘に参加しただけでした。日本は欧米向け、アジア向けの輸出を伸ばし、空前の好景気を迎えます。

戦争のために欧州諸国は、アジアに関与する余裕を失いました。それをチャンスと見た日本は、中国で

《第一次世界大戦》
パリ講和会議の様子
（国立国会図書館デジタルコレクション）

First Sino-Japanese War / Russo-Japanese War

When Japan opened up to the world in the late 19th century, the more economically and militarily advanced Western powers were expanding their colonies in Asia, Africa and elsewhere. The rulers of Meiji Japan thought that if the Korean Peninsula fell into the hands of a foreign power the safety of Japan would come under threat. It was over the control of Korea that Japan fought the Qing Empire (China) in the First Sino-Japanese War (1894-1895) and Russia in the Russo-Japanese War (1904-1905). Having won both wars, Japan annexed the Korean Empire in 1910 and made it a colony. Japan also gained stakes in Mainland China.

Japan's victory in the Russo-Japanese War inspired the nationalism of Asian peoples in showing that an Asian nation could defeat a strong Western country. India was under British colonial rule at the time and the Indian independence activist Jawaharlal Nehru stated that the Japanese victory was willingly welcomed by the peoples of Asia. However, he was critical regarding Japan's later actions, stating that, "the immediate result of it, however, was to add one more to the small group of aggressive, imperialistic powers."

World War I

In 1914, a war broke out between Germany and its allies and Great Britain and its allies. This was the beginning of World War I (1914-1918). Japan also entered the war under the Anglo-Japanese Alliance. However, due to the fact that the main theatres of combat were far away in Europe, Japan only participated in small-scale battles. Japan extended the reach of its exports to Europe and Asia and celebrated an unprecedented economic boom.

Because of the war the countries of Europe lost their ability to become heavily involved in Asia. Seeing this as a chance moment, Japan confronted the Chinese government with 21 demands in the interest of expanding Japan's interests there.

の権益拡大をねらって中国政府に21か条の要求を突きつけ、日中関係が悪化しました。欧州は戦争で荒廃します。日本は国際的地位を高め、1920年に設立された国際連盟では、常任理事国になりました。

【日中戦争／第二次世界大戦】

1929年の世界恐慌後、日本も深刻な不況に陥りました。中国では、欧米列強や日本に奪われていた権益を取り戻そうとする運動が高まっていました。

こうして外交、経済、社会の行き詰まりを、武力によって打破しようとする動きが力を持つようになり、1931年に満州（中国東北部）で日本軍により満州事変が引き起こされます。日本の主張が認められなかったため、日本は国際連盟から脱退しました。1937年には、日本は中国との全面戦争に突入します。中国の頑強な抵抗により戦争は長期化し、中国を支援する米英などとの関係も悪化していきました。

1939年、欧州で第二次世界大戦が始まると、日本は重要資源の確保と、欧米の中国に対する支援ルートの遮断をねらって、欧米の植民地であった東南アジアへの進出を強めます。その際、ドイツと同盟を結び、アメリカに対抗しようとしました。しかし、アメリカは日本の南進を認めず、日本への石油輸出を禁じます。日米交渉もまとまらず、1941年の日本軍のマレー半島上陸と真珠湾攻撃により、日本は米英などとの戦争に突入しました。そして、1945年に敗北します。戦場は、アジア・太平洋の広大な地域にわたり、各地で多くの犠牲を生みました。　　　　（土田宏成）

《第二次世界大戦》
日本政府の広報誌に掲載された真珠湾攻撃の様子
（JACAR（アジア歴史資料センター）Ref. A06031079700、写真週報（国立公文書館））

《第二次世界大戦》
砲弾製造に動員された女性たち
（JACAR（アジア歴史資料センター）Ref. A06031089700、写真週報（国立公文書館））

Sino-Japanese relations dramatically worsened as a result. Europe was devastated by the war. Japan, however, increased its international standing and became a permanent member of the League of Nations founded in 1920.

Second Sino-Japanese War / World War II

Japan fell into a serious economic depression after the Great Depression of 1929. A movement was growing in China too to regain those rights stolen from it by the Western Powers and Japan.

A move to break through this diplomatic, economic and social impasse through the use of force had gained support in Japan and in 1931 the Japanese army carried out the Mukden Incident in Inner Manchuria (North-East China). Japan's explanation for the Incident was not recognized by the League of Nations, so Japan abandoned its membership in the League. In 1937, Japan entered into full-scale war with China. Due to China's strong resistance, the war became prolonged and Japan's relations with the United States and Great Britain, which supported China, significantly worsened.

With the outbreak of WWII in Europe in 1939, Japan began to strengthen its expansion into Southeast Asia, which had been colonized by the West. It did so in order to secure important resources and cut off the assistance route between the Western powers and China. In order to do this, Japan signed an alliance pact with Germany and attempted to resist the United States. However, the United States did not recognize Japan's southern expansion and prohibited all oil exports to Japan. With US-Japan relations in chaos, the Japanese army invaded the Malay Peninsula and bombed Pearl Harbor, triggering a state of war between Japan and the United States and Great Britain. In 1945 Japan was defeated. The war took place over vast areas of the Asia-Pacific region and resulted in great human tragedy.

(Tr. M. Winchester)

【天皇】

　日本国は議会制民主主義に基づく立憲君主国で、天皇の地位は「日本国の象徴であり日本国民統合の象徴」であると日本国憲法に定められています。かつての大日本帝国憲法においては国家元首であり神聖で侵せない統治権の総攬者(そうらん)でした。天皇という呼称は、7世紀の律令制国家に遡ります。

　7世紀には、中華帝国と周辺の藩国が相互に依存し合う外交システムとしての冊封(さくほう)体制に動乱が起きました。朝鮮半島の高句麗・百済・新羅の抗争をめぐって、唐が新羅を支援する形で軍事介入し、新羅が半島を統一しました。

　一方、「倭王」は冊封体制から離脱し、自らを中心とした「天下」支配への志向を強めていきました。この「日本天皇」への転換をささえる神話として天神・日神の子孫としての天皇系譜を描く『古事記』『日本書紀』が編纂されました。このため日本の皇室は、世界の「もっとも古い世襲君主制」と言われています。

【沖縄】

　沖縄県は、日本国の最南端の県で、160の島で構成されています。そのうち、49島に人は住んでいますが、111島は無人島です。県庁所在地は沖縄本島の那覇市です。明治時代の琉球処分までは、中国大陸と薩摩藩との外交体制を保った琉球王国でした。

　琉球王国の文化遺産のうち、首里城、識名園(しきなえん)、斎場御嶽(セーファウタキ)など9か所は国連の世界遺産として登録されています。沖縄は亜熱帯のリゾート地として日本でもっとも人気のある観光地の1つでもあります。

世界遺産「識名園」
（写真提供：那覇市）

Emperor

Japan is a constitutional monarchy based upon parliamentary democracy and the position of the Emperor is stipulated in the Constitution of Japan as "the symbol of the State and the unity of the People." Previously, according to the Meiji-era Constitution of the Empire of Japan, the Emperor was the head of the Empire and exercised sacred and inviolable rights of sovereignty and legislative power. The appellation "Emperor" (*tennō*) dates back to the *Ritsu-ryō* state of the 7th century.

In the 7th century, the militarized vassal system through which the Chinese Empire and its surrounding kingdoms mutually supported each other experienced an upheaval. In the Korean Peninsula, the Tang Dynasty supported the Korean kingdom of Silla against those of Goguryeo and Baekje, thus allowing Silla to unite the Peninsula.

Meanwhile, in Japan, the "king of wa" withdrew from the vassal system, consolidating power "under heaven," and the genealogical myth concerning the "Japanese Emperor" as a descendent of Amaterasu-ōmikami was presented in the *Kojiki* (Records of Ancient Matters) and *Nihon Shoki* (Chronicles of Japan). For this reason, the Japanese Imperial Household is known as the world's "oldest hereditary monarchy."

Okinawa

Okinawa Prefecture is Japan's southernmost prefecture and consists of 160 individual islands. People inhabit 49 of these islands and 111 are uninhabited. The prefectural capital is Naha. Until the Ryūkyū disposal (*Ryūkyū shobun*) of the Meiji period, it was part of the Ryūkyū Kingdom maintaining diplomatic relations with both the Chinese mainland and the Satsuma Domain.

Cultural assets that date from the time of the Ryūkyū Kingdom include Shuri Castle, the gardens of Shikina-en, and the sacred spot of Sefa-utaki. These and 6 other sites are registered as UN World Heritage Sites. As a tropical resort, Okinawa is also known as one of Japan's most popular tourist

1945年、上陸した連合国軍と日本軍との間で行われた沖縄戦は多数の犠牲者を出しました。また、第二次世界大戦後、1972年まで沖縄はアメリカの占領下にありました。沖縄県の土地面積は、日本の全体の１％もないのにもかかわらず、現在も沖縄県に日本全国にある米軍施設の約74％が集中しています。

【アイヌ（先住民族）】

　アイヌ民族は、サハリン（樺太）島、北海道島、クリル（千島）列島、本州東北北部に生活してきた先住民族です。近代初頭、北海道島、クリル列島、サハリン島に暮らしていたアイヌが順に日本国民に統合されました。北海道島の入植植民地化の中、日本語の使用や生業転換を迫る政策が取られ、アイヌは少数者となりました。

　それ以前の暮らしは、多少の地域差はありますが、狩猟や漁撈、採集、農耕など複数の生業を組み合わせたものでした。周囲の民族との交易も不断に行い、精神文化はアニミズムを基調とし、シャーマニズムの要素も入っています。アイヌ語は孤立語です。

　近年のアイヌ政策によって、文化伝承に意欲を持っているアイヌが増えています。2008年６月に日本政府は、アイヌ民族は先住民族であることを認めました。しかし、植民地政策に遡るアイヌと和人（日本国の多数派民族のこと）との経済格差が依然としてあり、日本政府に「先住民族の権利に関する国際連合宣言」に適した政策が求められています。

（マーク・ウィンチェスター）

destinations.

In 1945, the Battle of Okinawa, which was conducted between Allied and Japanese forces, claimed a large number of victims. From the end of the Second World War until 1972, Okinawa remained under American military occupation. Despite the total land area of Okinawa Prefecture consisting of less than 1% of the whole of Japan, 74% of all American military facilities in Japan are concentrated on Okinawa.

Ainu (Indigenous Peoples)

The Ainu people are an Indigenous People who have lived in Sakhalin, Hokkaido Island, the Kuril Islands, and Northern Tōhoku. At the beginning of the modern era, Ainu who had been living on Hokkaido Island, the Kuril Islands and Sakhalin were, in turn, made into Japanese nationals. Within the context of settler colonialism in Hokkaido Island, policies aiming to transform traditional Ainu livelihood and develop the use of the Japanese language were introduced and the Ainu people became a minority within Japan.

While there are regional differences, the lifestyle of the Ainu people before this consisted of a combination of hunting, fishing, gathering and farming. They also constantly traded with other peoples in the region. Their traditional spiritual beliefs are based on a form of animism, and shamanism is also a factor. The Ainu language is a language isolate.

Due to recent Ainu policy, Ainu willing to take part in traditional cultural activities are increasing in number. In June 2008, the Japanese government recognized the Ainu people as an Indigenous People. However, economic disparity between Ainu and Wajin (non-Ainu ethnic Japanese), which dates back to colonial policy, still remains and the Japanese government has a responsibility to implement policy in line with the UN Declaration on the Rights of Indigenous Peoples.

(Mark Winchester)

アイヌから見た日本社会とは

　アイヌが日本社会をどのように見てきたかという問いには、困難がつきまといます。もともと隣接した地域に居住する、そして近代以降1つの国家を構成するアイヌと和人の異なる文化の接触は、14世紀に遡ります。一方、近世蝦夷地における和人支配の強化と近代北海道の入植植民地化、日本社会が歩んできた現代史とそれに伴ったアイヌの様々な近現代経験ゆえに、日本社会を見る「アイヌの視点」は（当然にも）一律に定められるものではありません。

　アイヌは、日本社会の構成員になっただけではなく、ときに同じ日本社会のあり方を擁護し、そしてときに、それを鋭く批判してきました。アイヌであることを理由に差別によって日本社会から排除され拒絶されるかもしれないという不安に常に苛まれているその経験は、日本の近代化を理解する上で北海道が欠かせないのと同じくらい、日本社会を理解するためには不可欠ではないでしょうか。だから、「アイヌから見た日本社会とは」ただ単純に日本社会そのものをそらさずに見るということを意味するのです。

　北の国境線を設けた日露和親条約締結（1855年）当時、地域住民にとって国境を引くのは普遍的な行為ではありませんでした。国家形成が直ちにアイヌにとって屈辱的なのではなく、そうなったのはその後にアイヌが国の正当な参画者として認められなかったからです。カムイ・アイヌ・シサムを一単位としてものを考えるアイヌ口承文学でしばしば問題となるのは、地政学的な力学ではなく、これらのバランスを崩す人間の非道です。歴史的に作り出された貧困が引き継がれていた1970年代にアイヌの小説家の鳩沢佐美夫が「アイヌ問題」を「アメリカの黒人問題」と並べて"人間に対する問題"と呼んだのも、この意味でも興味深いものです。

（マーク・ウィンチェスター）

Japanese Society from an Ainu Perspective

The question as to how Ainu people have viewed Japanese society throughout history is fraught with difficulty. Having lived in adjacent regions to begin with, contact between the different cultures of Ainu and Wajin, which, since the modern era, have come to make up those of a single state, dates back to the 14th century. Meanwhile, when we think about the strengthening of Wajin control over early-modern Ezochi, the settler-colonization of modern Hokkaido, and the more contemporary history that Japanese society has experienced to date, the diversity of Ainu modern and contemporary experience as a part of that history is vast. There is, of course, no uniform "Ainu point of view" concerning Japanese society.

Ainu not only became constitutive members of Japanese society, they have sometimes, quite naturally, been its greatest defenders, and sometimes its greatest critics. Their experiences have always been troubled by the fear that, because of discrimination due to their being Ainu, they would be excluded from and rejected by that society. These experiences are therefore perhaps as indispensible to understanding Japanese society as Hokkaido is to understanding Japan's modernization. In this sense, to talk about "Japanese Society from an Ainu Perspective" might just mean to look Japanese society straight in the face.

At the time the Treaty of Shimoda was signed between Japan and the Russian Empire deciding the northern borders of Japan, the setting of national borders was not a universal act for the people living in the region. The formation of the state was therefore not in itself humiliating for the Ainu people, but became so because afterwards Ainu were not fully recognized as legitimate participants in the country. In Ainu oral literature, which attempts to understand the world through the synthetic unit of *Kamuy* (everything with power that humans do not possess), *Ainu* (humans), and *Shisam* (Wajin), it is often not geopolitical power, but the cruelty of people that upsets this balance and which is brought into question. In this sense, it is of great interest that, in the context of the 1970s and the persistence of historically created poverty among Ainu, the Ainu novelist, Hatozawa Samio aligned the "Ainu problem" with that of "American blacks" and called it "a problem against humanity."

(Mark Winchester)

❖日本の世界文化遺産❖

富岡製糸場と絹産業遺産群
Tomioka Silk Mill and Related Sites

《明治時代以降の日本の生糸の大量生産に貢献》

　富岡製糸場は、養蚕技術の改良と教育機能を果たした２つの民間施設と、風穴を利用した蚕種(さんしゅ)貯蔵施設とが連携し、生糸の大量生産システムを確立しました。19世紀末期に養蚕・製糸業の革新に決定的な役割を果たすことで、日本が近代工業化世界に仲間入りする鍵となりました。製糸場の巨大建物は、西洋と日本の要素を結合させた日本特有の工場建築様式です。

【所在地】群馬県　【登録年】2014年
【写　真】東置繭所(ひがしおきまゆじょ)（提供：富岡市）

近現代の日本経済

The Modern and Contemporary Japanese Economy

三井本館（1929年竣工当時）（写真提供：三井不動産株式会社）

岩崎彌太郎（写真提供：公益財団法人三菱経済研究所付属三菱史料館）

【財閥】

　財閥とは、第二次世界大戦終結まで日本に存在した、複数の重要な産業において有力企業を傘下に有する事業体で、三井、三菱、住友が特に有名です。

　三井は、江戸時代の呉服商・両替商が起源で、三井物産に代表される商事部門が主力です。三菱は、幕末維新期の土佐藩の商会が起源で、岩崎彌太郎が初代社長であり、鉱業部門や造船業に代表される製造部門が主力です。そして、住友は、江戸時代の銅山経営が起源で、鉱業部門や化学工業が主力です。これらの財閥は、いずれも銀行部門も発展しており、傘下企業に対する資金供給を担っていました。

　また、1900年代以降、持株会社が傘下企業の株式を保有して統括するコンツェルン化が進みました。財閥は、第二次世界大戦後に経済民主化の一環でいずれも解体されましたが、かつての傘下企業は、現在も日本経済の発展に大きな役割を果たしています。

【総合商社】

　総合商社とは、日本に固有の商社の形態で、代表的な企業として、三菱商事、伊藤忠商事、三井物産、住友商事、丸紅などが知られています。

　総合商社が収益を得る主な方法は、①商品取引を仲介することによる口銭収入、②売買差益の獲得、③製造業、サービス業の事業運営による収入、④事業投資からの収入です。①は、メーカーから委託を受けた商社が商品を販売する際に、販売数量または販売価格の何％かを手数料として受け取ることです。②は、商社があらかじめ売値を決めずに仕入れ、市

Zaibatsu

A *zaibatsu* is a business entity that holds major companies in multiple important industries under its management, and which existed in Japan until the end of the Second World War. Mitsui, Mitsubishi and Sumitomo are particularly famous.

Mitsui originated from a dry goods dealer and money exchange business in the Edo period. Its core business was its commercial section, represented by the Mitsui trading company. Mitsubishi originated from a trading house in Tosa domain at the end of the Edo period, and was founded by Iwasaki Yatarō. Its core business was its mining and manufacturing sections, the latter represented by shipbuilding. Sumitomo originated from managing copper mines, and its core business was its mining section and chemical engineering. Each of these *zaibatsu* had also developed banking sections which were responsible for supplying funds for the companies under their management.

From the 1900s, business concerns developed, in which a holding company held stock in companies under its management and control. After the Second World War, the *zaibatsu* were dissolved as part of the process of economic democratization. However, the companies that formerly comprised *zaibatsu* continue to play a significant role in the development of the Japanese economy.

General Trading Company

A general trading company is a form of trading company that is unique to Japan. Representative enterprises are Mitsubishi Corporation, Itochu Corporation, Mitsui & Co., Ltd., Sumitomo Corporation, and Marubeni Corporation.

The main sources of revenue for a general trading company are as follows: ① commission income from mediating commodity trading, ② profits from sales margins, ③ income from business operations in the manufacturing and service industries, and ④ income from business investment. ① is when a trading company is commissioned to sell materials from a manufacture, whereupon the trading company receives a certain percentage of the sales amount or a price as a handling fee. ② is when a trading company buys something without deciding the selling price in advance, then sells it when the price of the market rises, thereby

場の価格が上がった段階で売り渡すことで、より高い収益を得ようとします。③は、商社が子会社を通して製造工程を担うことや、コンビニエンスストアの運営に関わることなどで得る収入です。ちなみに、ローソンは三菱商事、ファミリーマートは伊藤忠商事のそれぞれ子会社です。④は、資源開発等の商権の獲得や、収益の獲得を目的とした投資により得る収入です。

以上のように、総合商社は多種多様な事業を展開しており、日本経済の様々な分野に関わっています。

【トヨタ生産方式】

トヨタ自動車独自のトヨタ生産方式の基本思想は「徹底したムダの排除」であり、「ジャスト・イン・タイム」と「自働化」を二本柱とし、カローラなどの多様な車種が生産されています。

初代カローラKE10型
（写真提供：トヨタ博物館）

「ジャスト・イン・タイム」とは、1台の自動車を流れ作業で組み立てる過程で、必要な部品が、必要な時に、必要なだけ、生産ラインの脇に到着するようにすることです。「かんばん」と呼ばれるカードに、部品の引き取りや運搬、生産指示に関する情報が示され、工場内を行き来させて管理しています。

「自働化」とは、不良品の生産や機械の故障を自動的にチェックし、異常時には自動停止する仕組みです。この仕組みの特徴は、異常でストップした時に初めて人間が駆けつけることで、1人で何台もの機械を受け持ち、生産効率を向上させられると共に、不良品を作り続けないことにあります。

このような特徴を持つトヨタ生産方式は、現在も改良が続けられています。　　　　　　　　（神谷久覚）

seeking to obtain a higher profit. ③ is the income earned from a trading company taking charge of manufacturing processes through subsidiaries, and is related to the operation of convenience stores. By the way, Lawson is a subsidiary of Mitsubishi Corporation and Family Mart is a subsidiary of Itochu Corporation. Finally, ④ is the income earned by acquiring commercial rights such as resource development, and investment aimed at earnings.

As the above shows, general trading companies encompass diverse businesses, and are connected to various fields in the Japanese economy.

Toyota Production System

The principle of Toyota Motor Corporation's Proprietary Toyota Production System is the "thorough elimination of waste," and it is founded on the twin pillars of "just in time" and "automation." It has been used to manufacture many makes of car, such as the Corolla.

"Just in time" refers to a system that makes necessary parts arrive at the necessary time, and in the necessary amounts, in the production line used in the process of manufacturing a car through a flow operation. Information about unloading or transporting parts, as well as production instructions, are indicated on cards called *kanban*, and the system is managed through the coming and going of these cards.

"Automation" refers to a system that checks the production of defective products and machine problems automatically, and stops production automatically when something goes wrong. This system is characterized by one person being in charge of many machines, and not requiring human intervention until it needs to be stopped due to a problem. This increases manufacturing efficiency as well as preventing the production of defective products.

Even today, improvements continue to be made to the Toyota Production System. (Tr. A. T. Kamei-Dyche)

15｜近現代の日本経済

【産業革命】

大阪紡績会社の工場
（写真提供：東洋紡株式会社）

産業革命とは、分業と協業により、機械を用いて大量生産される生産方式が普及・定着する過程です。イギリスでは、18世紀後半から紡績業で産業革命が進み、日本では1880年代以降産業革命が本格化しました。日本の産業革命の特徴は、イギリスやフランスから、最先端の技術を導入できたことです。しかし、イギリスやフランスなどの製品が大量に輸入されるため、日本での機械生産は不利な状況でした。

日本の産業革命は、紡績業や製糸業などの軽工業から始まり、やがて造船業や鉄鋼業などの重工業も発展しました。多数の出資者から資金を集めて設立される株式会社が増加する過程では、渋沢栄一が大きな役割を果たしました。

産業革命の進展は日本の経済発展と密接に関連していますが、紡績業や製糸業の低いコストによる生産は、女性労働者の低賃金かつ長時間の労働により実現されていたことも見逃せない事実です。

渋沢栄一（写真提供：渋沢史料館）

【高度成長】

高度成長とは、急激な経済成長のことです。日本では、1956-70年の平均経済成長率が約10％を記録しました。日本の高度成長の主な理由は、第1に、企業が活発に設備投資を行い、銀行が企業への融資に積極的だったこと、第2に、資源価格が低水準で推移したこと、第3に、1960年代後半以降、自動車産業を中心として輸出が急速に拡大したことです。

1950年代後半には、白黒テレビ、洗濯機、電気冷蔵庫のいわゆる「三種の神器」、1960年代後半には、

カラーテレビ（1960年製）（写真提供：東芝未来博物館）

Industrial Revolution

The Industrial Revolution is the process whereby mass production through the use of machines was established and spread through collaboration and the division of labor. In the United Kingdom the Industrial Revolution progressed in the spinning industry from the latter half of the 18th century, and in Japan it came to take off from the 1880s. The particular characteristic of Japan's Industrial Revolution is that it was able to produce cutting-edge technology from the United Kingdom and France. However, production using machines in Japan was at a disadvantage because products made in the United Kingdom or France were imported in large quantities.

The Industrial Revolution in Japan began with light industry such as the spinning and silk-reeling industries, and eventually heavy industry such as the shipbuilding and steel industries also developed. Shibusawa Eiichi played a significant role in the process of increasing the number of joint stock companies, which were established by collecting funds from a large number of investors.

While the progress of the Industrial Revolution was intertwined with the economic development of Japan, it is important to note that the low-cost production in the spinning and silk-reeling industries was realized by women workers who worked long hours for low wages.

High Growth

High growth refers to rapid economic growth. In Japan, the average economic growth rate during the period from 1956 to 1970 was recorded at about 10%. The main reasons for the high growth in Japan were as follows: first, firms actively invested in capital investment, and banks were active in financing companies; second, resource prices transitioned at low levels; and third, since the latter half of the 1960s, exports expanded rapidly, especially in the automobile industry.

In the latter half of the 1950s, there were the so-called "three sacred treasures" —— a black-and-white television, a washing machine, and an electric refrigerator —— and then in the latter half of the 1960s the "3 Cs" —— a color television, air

カラーテレビ、クーラー、自動車のいわゆる「3C」が普及し、家庭生活も大きく変化しました。スーパーマーケットでの買い物が一般化し、消費のあり方にも変化が現われました。さらに、高速道路網の広がりや東海道新幹線の開業は、ヒトとモノの移動を活発にしました。

高度成長は、為替相場が円高ドル安になったことや、第4次中東戦争で原油価格が高騰したことが主な原因となって、1974年に経済成長率がマイナスを記録し、終わりました。

東海道新幹線の開業式(1964年)（Ⓒ交通新聞社）

【バブル経済】

バブル経済とは、株式や土地などの資産価格が上昇し、経済が実態以上に泡のように膨張した状態のことです。日本では、1985年のプラザ合意をきっかけに円高ドル安が進み、輸出企業の不振による不況を防ぐために日本銀行が公定歩合を引き下げ、金融緩和を行いました。このため、民間金融機関が企業への融資を増やし、経済活動が活発になり、東京証券取引所では株式取引が活発に行われました。

しかし、1989年5月に日本銀行が公定歩合を引き上げて金融引締めに転じると、1989年末に戦後最高の38,900円台を記録した日経平均株価は、翌年末には23,800円台にまで下落しました。また、1990年3月に、大蔵省の通達で不動産業向けの融資の抑制が図られると、地価が下落に転じました。

株式や土地を主な担保として企業に融資していた金融機関は、不良債権を大量に抱え、その処理に多額の税金が費やされるなど、バブル経済崩壊による影響は大きかったのです。　　　　　（神谷久覚）

東京証券取引所立会場(1980年代後半)（写真提供：株式会社日本取引所グループ）

conditioner, and a car — which became common, and home life also changed significantly. Shopping at supermarkets became commonplace, and changes appeared in the patterns of consumption. Additionally, the expansion of the highway network and the opening of the Tokaido Shinkansen expanded the movement of people and goods.

High growth in Japan ended with a year of negative economic growth in 1974, largely due to the appreciation of the Yen against the US Dollar on the exchange market, and the rising prices of crude oil due to the fourth Arab-Israeli War.

Bubble Economy

A bubble economy is a situation in which asset prices, such as those of stocks and land, are rising and the economy expands like a bubble beyond the actual economic situation. In Japan, following the Plaza Accord in 1985, the Yen continued to appreciate against the US Dollar, prompting the Bank of Japan to implement monetary easing and reduce the official discount rate in order to prevent a depression caused by the slump in export enterprises. As a result, private financial institutions increased loans to companies, economic activity became more vigorous, and stock trading on the Tokyo Stock Exchange intensified.

However, when the Bank of Japan raised the official discount rate in May 1989 and began to tighten monetary policy, the Nikkei Stock Average, which recorded its highest postwar value at 38,900 Yen at the end of 1989, fell to just 23,800 Yen by the end of the following year. Then, in March 1990, land prices began to drop as the Ministry of Finance aimed at suppressing financing for the real estate industry.

Financial institutions that had financed companies in exchange for land and stocks as collateral had large amounts of bad debt and a large amount of tax was spent on disposal. In this way, the impact of the economic collapse of the bubble economy was enormous. (Tr. A. T. Kamei-Dyche)

GDPの算出方法と日本の現状

　新聞やテレビのニュースなどでGDPという言葉を目にすることは多いと思います。ここでは、GDPがどのように算出されるかを考えてみましょう。

　GDPとは、Gross Domestic Productの略で、日本語では「国内総生産」と訳されます。GDPは、「国内で一定期間（1年、四半期など）に生産された付加価値（新しく創出した価値）の総額」であり、生産面から一国の経済規模を示す代表的指標です。国際連合が定めた統一基準に従って計測・推測され、公表されます。

　GDPは生産された付加価値の総額であり、誰かに購入されると付加価値に対する支出が行われます。計算式は以下の通りです。

　　GDP＝民間需要＋公的需要＋純輸出

　民間需要とは、家計部門と企業部門による支出の合計であり、主に個人消費、住宅投資、企業による設備投資が該当します。公的需要とは、政府による支出の合計であり、主に道路の建設に代表される公共投資が該当します。純輸出は、輸出額から輸入額を差し引いて求められます。

　以上のような方法で算出されるGDPですが、2020年度の日本の名目GDPは536.6兆円です。名目GDPとは実際の数値であり、これに対して、物価変動の影響を取り除いた数値を実質GDPと言います。名目GDPの内訳は、民間需要が73.0％、公的需要が27.0％です。注目すべきは、名目GDP全体に占める家計部門の消費支出の割合が51.8％であり、個人消費の増減が、GDPの動向に及ぼす影響が大きいことです。日本経済の今後の成長のカギは、家計部門の消費支出が握っているのかもしれません。

　なお、日本の名目GDP（2020年）は、アメリカ、中国に次ぐ世界第3位です。

（神谷久覚）

How to Calculate GDP, and Japan's Current Situation

You have likely seen the term "GDP" in newspapers or on TV news on many occasions. Let's think about how GDP is calculated.

GDP is an abbreviation for Gross Domestic Product, which refers to "the gross amount of the added value (i.e., newly-produced value) that was produced domestically within a certain period of time (such as a year, or a quarter)." It is a benchmark that indicates the economic scale of a nation based on its production. It is measured and surmised according to a unified standard set by the United Nations, and is publically released.

Since the GDP is the gross amount of the added value of products and services, if those are purchased by someone then the expense will be paid for the added value. The formula is as follows:

GDP = private-sector demand + public demand + net exports

Private-sector demand refers to the total expense by the household sector and the enterprise sector. This mainly corresponds to individual consumption, housing investment, and capital investment by enterprises. Public demand refers to the total expenses of a government, and mainly corresponds to public investment represented by the construction of roads. Net exports are calculated by subtracting the import value from the export value.

When we calculate GDP using the above method, we see that Japan's nominal GDP in fiscal 2020 was 536.6 trillion Yen. Nominal GDP is the actual number; on the other hand, real GDP is what we call the number after eliminating the influence of fluctuation in prices. The breakdown of nominal GDP is 73.0% private sector, and 27.0% public sector. The notable point is that the percentage of the household sector constitutes 51.8% of the total nominal GDP, and increases or decreases in individual consumption have a large impact on GDP trends. Consumption expenses of the household sector may well be the key to future economic growth in Japan.

Additionally, Japan's nominal GDP (2020 figures) is the third in the world, after the US and China.

(Tr. A. T. Kamei-Dyche)

❖日本の世界文化遺産❖

⓯ 明治日本の産業革命遺産
〜鉄鋼・製鋼、造船、石炭産業〜

Sites of Japan's Meiji Industrial Revolution
〜 Iron and Steel, Shipbuilding and Coal Mining 〜

《日本の近代化の礎となった産業遺産群》

　19世紀後半から20世紀初頭、日本が欧米から導入した技術を国内の需要や伝統に適合するよう改良したもので、日本が短期間で世界有数の産業国家になった過程を物語る23の産業遺産群です。製鉄・鉄鋼、造船、石炭という基幹産業において、非西洋国家で初めて産業国家化に成功した偉業です。

　【所在地】山口県・鹿児島県・静岡県・岩手県・佐賀県・長崎県・
　　　　　　福岡県・熊本県　【登録年】2015年
　【写　真】萩反射炉（提供：萩市観光協会）

16
現代日本の政治
Politics in Contemporary Japan

【日本国憲法】

　日本国憲法は、1946年に公布、1947年に施行されました。国民主権、基本的人権の尊重、平和主義の3つを基本原則としています。

　日本国憲法は、第二次世界大戦の敗戦後、連合国軍の占領下で進められた改革で、大日本帝国憲法の改正により成立しました。天皇は政治的な権力を持たない、日本国・日本国民統合の象徴とされました。日本国憲法により、日本は天皇中心の国から、国民中心の国に大きく変わったのです。

　戦争放棄・戦力不保持を定めた第9条は、日本国憲法の特徴です。戦争に対する反省が示されています。ただし、自衛権は否定していないものとされ、のちに自衛隊が設置されました。

　日本国憲法については、戦後日本の平和と民主主義を守ってきたという意見がある一方で、占領下で押し付けられたものとする意見もあります。憲法は制定以来、1度も改正されていませんが、国内外の環境変化に合わせて改正すべきだという議論も高まってきています。

日本国憲法（国立公文書館デジタルアーカイブ）

【内閣制度】

　内閣制度は、明治時代の1885年にヨーロッパの制度を参考に導入されました。内閣のトップが内閣総理大臣で、日本を代表する政治家です。

　第二次世界大戦後、日本国憲法によって国民主権の原則が確立されてからは、内閣総理大臣は国会議員の中から、国会の議決によって指名され、天皇によって任命されることになりました。内閣は行政権を担

The Constitution of Japan

The Constitution of Japan was promulgated in 1946 and took effect in 1947. Popular sovereignty, respect for fundamental human rights, and pacifism are its three basic principles.

The Constitution of Japan was written under the allied occupation after Japan's defeat in World War II. It entirely revised the Constitution of the Empire of Japan. The Emperor was made a symbol of the state and the unity of the people without political power. Thus, with the promulgation of the Constitution of Japan, Japan became a country with the people (Japanese nationals, *kokumin*) at the center of its polity — a position previously held by the Emperor.

Article 9, which stipulates the renunciation of war and maintenance of war potential, is another feature of the Constitution. It reflects feelings of remorse toward war. However, it is also understood that the Constitution does not deny the right to self-defense and Japan's Self-Defense Force was subsequently established.

While many are of the opinion that the Constitution of Japan has protected postwar Japan's peace and democracy, there are also people with the opinion that it was forced upon Japan by the occupation authorities. The Constitution has never been revised since its promulgation and there is growing debate over whether it should be revised in accordance with the changing domestic and international order.

The Cabinet System

The cabinet system was introduced to Japan in 1885 during the Meiji period with reference to similar systems in Europe. At the top of the Cabinet is the Prime Minister, the politician who represents Japan.

After World War II and the establishment of popular sovereignty as a principle of the Constitution of Japan, the Prime Minister came to be nominated and voted upon by the members of the Diet and then appointed by the Emperor. The cabinet is responsible for administrative authority and bears responsibility

い、国会に対し連帯して責任を負います。日本は議院内閣制の国です。

内閣は、内閣総理大臣と内閣総理大臣によって任命される国務大臣の20人弱で構成されています。国務大臣の過半数は国会議員から選ばれます。

1990年代、グローバル化と、バブル経済崩壊後の厳しい社会経済情勢に対応するため、内閣総理大臣の権限と指導力の強化が求められ、2000年頃から制度改革が実施されました。よって、現在の内閣総理大臣は、以前よりもリーダーシップが発揮しやすくなっています。

【地方制度】

日本には47の都道府県と約1700の市町村があります。都道府県には、住民の選挙によって選ばれる知事と議会が置かれています。市町村にも同様に市町村長と議会が置かれています。

首都である東京都の中心部には23の特別区があります。それ以外にも人口50万人以上の大都市のうちで有力な市は、政令指定都市として、都道府県に準じた権限を持っています。

日本の地方制度は長らく中央集権的でしたが、地方が主体的に地域の問題に取り組み、個性を発揮できるように、地方に権限を移す地方分権が進められています。

東京などの大都市部への若者の流出により、地方は過疎化と高齢化に苦しんでいます。地方をどのように活性化するかは、日本が抱える課題の1つです。

（土田宏成）

to work in solidarity with the Diet. Japan is a country with a parliamentary cabinet system.

The cabinet is made up the Prime Minister and less than 20 state secretaries appointed by the Prime Minister. The majority of state secretaries are elected from among Diet members.

In order to deal with demanding socioeconomic conditions since the collapse of the bubble economy and the emergence of globalization in the 1990s, many demanded the power of the Prime Minister be increased and around the year 2000, institutional reforms were carried out. Accordingly, the Prime Minister today is more likely to display leadership than before.

Regional Government

There are 47 prefectures and 1700 municipalities in Japan. In each prefecture there are governors and regional parliaments that are chosen through resident elections. Municipal mayors and parliaments are also elected in the same way.

There are 23 districts in the center of the capital Tokyo. As cities designated by government ordinance, large cities with populations of over 500,000, have authority equivalent to that of prefectures.

Regional government in Japan had long been centralized. However, transferring authority to regional assemblies through local decentralization is underway in order that regional districts can actively address regional issues on their own initiative and demonstrate their individuality.

Due to the flow of young people to large metropolitan areas such as Tokyo, Japan's regions are suffering from depopulation and an aging society. The challenge of how to revitalize Japan's regions is a major issue for the country today.

(Tr. M. Winchester)

国会議事堂(写真提供:参議院事務局)

【国会】

　日本の議会は、「国会」と呼ばれ、衆議院と参議院から構成される二院制です。日本国憲法で「国権の最高機関」と位置づけられています。国会は立法権と予算議決権を持ち、内閣総理大臣は国会議員の中から国会の議決で指名されます。

　予算の議決や総理大臣の指名など、重要案件については衆議院の決定が優越しますが、それ以外については、参議院は衆議院と同等の権限を持っています。二院制により、慎重な審議がなされることが期待されています。

　国会には、常会（毎年1月中に召集される）と、臨時会、特別会（衆議院の解散・総選挙直後に開かれる）があり、会期が限定されています。会期中に議決されなかった案件は、特別な場合を除いて、廃案になります。そこで、会期末になると、重要案件を議決しようとする与党と、それに反対し、時間切れに持ち込もうとする野党の対立が激化します。

【選挙】

　1889年に大日本帝国憲法が制定され、日本に議会政治が導入され、1890年に第1回衆議院議員総選挙が実施されました。しかし、選挙権を持つのは25歳以上の男子で、納税額による制限もありました。その後、納税額の基準は段階的に引き下げられます。第一次世界大戦後には、世界的な民主化の影響を受け、日本でも普通選挙を求める運動が高まり、1925年に納税額による制限は撤廃されました。女性参政権を求める運動も行われましたが、第二次世界大戦

The National Diet

The Japanese parliament is called the 'Diet' and is a bicameral legislative system. It has a lower House of Representatives and upper House of Councilors. It is considered to be the 'highest order of state power' under the Constitution of Japan. Diet members in the parliamentary assembly nominate the Prime Minister, who has legislative rights and budget setting authority.

The House of Representatives decision will dominate in important matters such as budget decisions and the nomination of Prime Minister. For other decisions, the House of Councilors has the same authority as the House of Representatives. It is expected that careful deliberation on legislative matters will take place between the two Houses.

The Diet has ordinary sessions (convened in January each year), extraordinary sessions, and special sessions (held after the dissolution of the House of Representatives and directly after general elections). The duration of each session is limited. Items that are not voted upon during each session will be abandoned except in special circumstances. Therefore, at the end of each session, conflict intensifies between the ruling parties attempting to vote on what they see as important and the opposition parties attempting to introduce new items before the time limit expires.

Elections

The Constitution of the Empire of Japan was proclaimed in 1889 and parliamentary politics were introduced to Japan. The first general election of the House of Representatives was held in 1890. However, voting rights were granted only to men over the age of 25 and there were also restrictions that came into effect depending on the amount of tax paid. These tax restrictions were gradually reduced. After World War I, a people's movement demanding common elections emerged in Japan and was influenced by global moves toward democratization. In 1925, tax restrictions were abolished. There were also movements demanding votes for women, however their aim was not realized until after World War II.

前には実現しませんでした。

　1945年、第二次世界大戦の敗戦後、連合国軍の占領下で、日本の民主化が進められました。同年12月には選挙法が改正され、選挙権が20歳以上の男女に与えられ、1946年の選挙では女性議員も誕生しました。

　こうして政治参加が拡大してきましたが、日本の女性政治家の数は、世界最低レベルです。投票率の低下（特に若い世代で顕著）も問題となっています。2015年には、若者の政治参加を促進するため、選挙権年齢を、世界の多くの国々と同様に18歳に引き下げる選挙法改正が行われました。

投票箱と記載台（写真提供：千葉市稲毛区役所）

【政党】

　日本には複数の政党があります。自由民主党（自民党）は、1955年の結党以来、約4年を除いて政権を担当し続けています。こうした現象は、自由主義体制をとる国ではめずらしいことです。自民党がこれほど長期にわたって政権を維持できた理由としては、高度経済成長を実現し、日本を経済大国にしたこと、社会保障制度の整備も行ってきたことなどが挙げられます。

　自民党に対抗し政権を担当できる政党をつくるために1998年に民主党が結成され、2009年から2012年まで政権を担当しました。

　現在は自民党の他に、立憲民主党、日本維新の会、公明党、国民民主党、日本共産党などがあります。一方、支持政党を持たない無党派層の割合も増えています。

（土田宏成）

After Japan's defeat in World War II in 1945, the democratization of Japan was promoted under the allied occupation. In December 1945, the election law was revised and the right to vote was given to all men and women over 20 years old. Japan's first female politicians were also elected in 1946.

Political participation thus expanded, however, the number of female politicians in Japan remains among the world's lowest. Declining voter turnout (particularly among younger generations) has also become a problem. In 2015, in order to promote the political participation of young people, the election law was changed and voting age in Japan was lowered to 18 years old; similar to many other countries around the world.

Political Parties

There are many political parties in Japan. The Liberal Democratic Party (LDP) has been consistently in charge of Japan's administration since its inauguration in 1955 (except for around 4 years). This phenomenon is unusual in countries with a liberal political system. Reasons for why the LDP has managed to maintain political power for such a long period include positive public evaluation of high economic growth, the establishment of Japan as a major economy, and improvements to the social security system that have been made under LDP leadership.

The Democratic Party was formed in 1998 to challenge the LDP and create an opposition party capable of running an administration. It achieved this aim, taking charge of Japan from 2009 until 2012. In addition to the LDP there are the Constitutional Democratic Party of Japan, the Japan Innovation Party, Komeito, the Democratic Party For the People, and the Japanese Communist Party. The proportion of non-partisan politicians who do not support a particular political party has also grown in size.

(Tr. M. Winchester)

戦後日本の政治と外交

　第二次世界大戦後の日本の骨格は、連合国軍（事実上、アメリカ軍）の占領下で進められた改革によって形成されました。そして冷戦が、戦後日本のあり方を規定します。アメリカの占領下にあった日本は、自由主義陣営に組み込まれることになりました。1951年に日本は、自由主義国を中心とする国々との間でサンフランシスコ平和条約を結び、独立を回復します。同時に日米安全保障条約も締結され、独立回復後も米軍が日本に駐留することになりました。

　1955年に結成された自由民主党の長期政権下で、日本は高度経済成長を遂げ、経済大国と呼ばれるようになります。自由主義陣営の一国として、アメリカとの同盟関係を重視しつつ、日本は社会主義国との関係改善も模索し、1956年にはソ連と、1972年には中国と国交を正常化します。他方、日本の植民地支配から独立した韓国とは、1965年に国交を正常化しました。

　1990年前後に冷戦は終結、グローバル化が進展します。同じ頃、日本経済はバブルの発生と崩壊を経験し、その後長期低迷に入りました。1995年には阪神・淡路大震災、2011年には東日本大震災・福島原発事故と、巨大災害にも襲われます。少子高齢化も進みました。一方でこの間、中国は大きく経済発展を遂げ、その存在感を増していきました。

　1990年代半ば頃から、北朝鮮による核開発問題が起こります。2002年の「日朝平壌宣言」により日本と北朝鮮は国交正常化に向けた交渉をすることにしましたが、北朝鮮による日本人拉致問題、核開発問題は未解決で、国交も結ばれていません。　　（土田宏成）

Postwar Japan's Politics and Foreign Relations

The framework of postwar Japan was created by the reforms advanced under the occupation forces of the allied powers (effectively the US military). Furthermore, the Cold War prescribed how postwar Japan would develop. Japan, under the occupation of the United States, was incorporated into the liberal camp. In 1951, Japan regained independence through concluding the San Francisco Peace Treaty predominantly with states that belonged to this liberal group. Alongside this, the US-Japan Security Treaty was signed leading to American troops remaining in Japan after independence.

Under the long-term administration of the Liberal Democratic Party formed in 1955, Japan achieved high-speed economic growth and became known as a major economic power. As a member of the liberal camp, Japan, while stressing its bilateral alliance with the US, also sought to improve its relations with the socialist bloc. Diplomacy was normalized with the Soviet Union in 1956 and with the Peoples Republic of China in 1972. Relations with the Republic of Korea, which had gained independence from Japanese colonial rule, were normalized in 1965.

The Soviet Union and the Eastern European socialist bloc collapsed around the year 1990 and the Cold War ended leading to an era of globalization. During the same period, the Japanese economy experienced the birth and burst of a bubble economy and entered a long period of uncertainty. Huge disasters such as the Great Hanshin Earthquake of 1995 and the Great East Japan Earthquake and Fukushima nuclear power plant accident of 2011 also hit Japan in this period. Japan's declining birthrate and aging population intensified. Meanwhile, China achieved great economic advancement and an increased global presence.

The nuclear development issue of the Democratic Peoples Republic of Korea also began in the late 1990s. Japan and North Korea had decided to negotiate toward the normalization of diplomatic relations according to the 2002 Japan-North Korea Pyongyang Declaration; however, the issue of the abduction of Japanese citizens by North Korea and the North's development of nuclear weapons remain unresolved and diplomatic relations between Japan and North Korea have not been established.

(Tr. M. Winchester)

❖日本の世界文化遺産❖

⑯ ル・コルビュジエの建築作品
～近代建築運動への顕著な貢献～

*The Architectural Work of Le Corbusier,
an Outstanding Contribution to the Modern Movement*

《近代建築運動への顕著な貢献》

　パリを拠点に活躍した建築家・都市計画家ル・コルビュジエの作品のうち三大陸7か国（フランス・日本・ドイツ・スイス・ベルギー・アルゼンチン・インド）にある17資産で構成された世界遺産。国立西洋美術館もその1つ。建築史上初めて、建築の実践が全地球規模のものとなったことを示し、近代の社会的、人間的ニーズに対応した建築の新しいコンセプトを反映しています。

【登録年】2016年
【写　真】国立西洋美術館（提供：国立西洋美術館）

17

現代日本の外交・安全保障

Foreign Policy and Security in Contemporary Japan

17 | 現代日本の外交・安全保障

【自衛隊】

　自衛隊は、日本の平和と独立を守り、国の安全を保つため、日本を防衛することを主たる任務とする組織です。自衛隊の定員は約25万人（現員は約22万5千人）で、陸上自衛隊、海上自衛隊、航空自衛隊の3つに分かれています。

　自衛隊の前身は、1950年の朝鮮戦争勃発後に設置された警察予備隊です。自衛隊は、1954年に発足しました。憲法9条では、戦争放棄と戦力不保持が定められていますが、自衛権は否定していないとされ、自衛隊は自衛のための必要最小限度の実力と説明されてきました。しかし、やはり憲法違反ではないかという意見もあります。

　自衛隊は国防のための組織ですが、災害の多い日本では災害時の救助活動にも大きな役割を果たします。国民のためのそうした活動が評価され、現在、多くの国民が自衛隊によい印象を持っています。

東日本大震災における災害派遣活動（陸上自衛隊HPより引用）

　経済大国になった日本は、1990年代に入ると、より大きな国際貢献を求められるようになりました。経済的貢献だけでなく人的貢献も求められ、自衛隊は国連のPKOに参加したり、多国籍軍に協力したりするために、海外に派遣されるようになります。

　近年の巨大災害の発生や安全保障環境の変化により、自衛隊の役割は拡大しています。平和主義を堅持しながら日本の安全を守るために、自衛隊の活動はどうあるべきか、議論が行われています。

【日米同盟】

　アメリカは、日本にとって最も重要な同盟国です。

Japan Self-Defense Forces

The Japan Self-Defense Forces (JSDF) is an organization whose main duty is to defend Japan in order to preserve its peace and independence and to maintain the security of the country. The capacity of the JSDF consists of 250,000 regular staff (currently 225,000) divided into the Ground Self-Defense Force, the Maritime Self-Defense Force and the Air Self-Defense Force.

The direct predecessor of the JSDF is the National Police Reserve. This was set up after the outbreak of the Korean War in 1950. The JSDF was established in 1954. Article 9 of the Constitution of Japan stipulates that the Japanese people renounce war and the maintenance of military forces. However, it is understood that the right to self-defense has not been denied under the Constitution and the JSDF is justified in maintaining the minimum necessary force for self-defense. There are nevertheless some people with the opinion that the JSDF exists in violation of the Constitution.

The JSDF is an organization for national defense; however, they also play a large role in disaster relief in Japan. Such activities have left many citizens in Japan with a good impression of the JSDF.

Having become a significant economic power in the world, greater international contributions by Japan have come to be expected. This is especially so since the 1990s. Not only economic but human contributions have come to be expected and this has led to the JSDF being dispatched abroad as part of United Nations peacekeeping operations and cooperation with multinational military operations.

Due to the recent occurrence of large-scale disasters in Japan and the changing security environment, the role of the JSDF is expanding. How the JSDF can protect Japan's security at the same time as adhering to state pacifism is the subject of keen debate.

The US-Japan Alliance

The United States of America is Japan's most important ally.

日米の同盟関係の基礎となっているのが、1951年に結ばれた日米安全保障条約で、同条約に基づいて、アメリカ軍が日本に駐留しています。

通常の同盟では、両者は同等の義務を負います。しかし、日米同盟は違っています。日本がどこかの国に攻撃を受けた場合、アメリカは日本とともに戦いますが、アメリカに同様のことがあっても、日本は憲法上、集団的自衛権が制限されており、限られた場合にしか、アメリカとともに戦うことはできません。アメリカが軍隊を提供するのに対して、日本は基地を提供するというのが、同盟の基本構造になっています。

自衛のための必要最小限の実力である自衛隊と、アメリカの強大な軍事力の組合せによって、日本に対する侵略を抑止することが、日本の安全保障戦略の基本です。

【国際連合】

第二次世界大戦の敗戦国であった日本が80番目の加盟国として、国際連合への加盟を認められたのは、1956年のことでした。以後、日本は、戦争に対する反省をもとに、財政面のみならず、国連の関わる平和・安全、経済・社会・文化、人道などのあらゆる分野で貢献をしてきました。

こうした活動が認められ、日本は国連安全保障理事会の非常任理事国（任期2年）に加盟国で最多の11回選出されています。2017年末に11回目の任期が終わりましたが、2022年におこなわれる安保理非常任理事国選挙への立候補を発表しています。日本は、さらに国際社会において重要な責任を果たすために、安保理常任理事国入りを目指しています。（土田宏成）

The 1951 Treaty of Mutual Cooperation and Security between the United States and Japan forms the basis of US-Japan relations and the US military is stationed in Japan in accordance with the treaty.

In a normal alliance between nations, both nations have equal duties to one another. However, the US-Japan alliance is different. If Japan is attacked by another country, the US will fight with Japan, but if the US faces the same threat, the right to collective self-defense is limited under the Japanese Constitution. There are only a few circumstances in which Japan could fight alongside the US. The basic structure of the US-Japan alliance consists of the US providing troops to Japan, and Japan providing them with military bases.

The foundation of Japan's security strategy to deter any potential invasion of the country consists of a combination of the vast military might of the US and the minimum necessary force needed to protect Japan provided by the JSDF.

The United Nations

In 1956, Japan, a defeated country in World War II, was recognized as the 80th member state of the United Nations. Since then, and on reflection of Japan's role in WWII, Japan has made contributions not only financially, but in all of the fields the United Nations is concerned: peace, security, the economy, society, culture, and humanitarian causes.

Thanks to these activities, Japan has been elected 11 times to serve as a non-permanent member of the UN Security Council (each consisting of a 2 year term). This is the most frequent number of terms served by any UN non-permanent member state. At the end of 2017 Japan's 11th term ended but Japan's candidacy for the election of non-permanent members of the UN security council due to take part in 2022 has been announced.

(Tr. M. Winchester)

【日中】

　中国は、日本の戦争によって、最も深刻な影響をうけた国の1つです。第二次世界大戦後、中国では国民党と共産党の内戦が再燃し、1949年に中国共産党が大陸に中華人民共和国を樹立し、国民党政権は台湾に逃れ、互いに中国の正統政府を名乗りました。

　冷戦下、1952年に日本は台湾の国民党政権を中国の正統政府と認め、平和条約を締結します。しかし、1972年には日中共同声明によって中華人民共和国と国交を結び、台湾とは断交しました。1978年には日中平和友好条約が結ばれ、日中関係は経済を中心に発展していきます。日本からのODAもあり、中国は急速な経済発展を遂げ、日本企業も中国に進出、中国は日本にとって最大の貿易相手国になりました。

　21世紀に入り、中国のGDPは日本を抜き、世界第2位となり、国際的にその存在感を増しています。日中間には、戦争に関わる歴史問題、また、尖閣諸島をめぐる問題などがあります。しかし、日中関係は、日中相互にとってのみならず、世界に影響を与える重要な二国間関係です。両国はそのことを認識し、世界の未来を考えた外交をする必要があります。

【日韓】

　1910年、韓国併合条約により日本は韓国（大韓帝国）を植民地化しました。その後、日本の統治は、1945年の日本の敗戦まで続きます。1948年、冷戦の影響により、朝鮮半島の北側に社会主義国の朝鮮民主主義人民共和国（北朝鮮）、南側に自由主義国の大韓民国（韓国）が建国され、1950年には朝鮮戦争

Japan-China Relations

China is a country that was influenced severely by war with Japan. After World War II, civil war resumed between the Nationalist Party (Kuomintang) and the Communist Party. In 1949, the Chinese Communist Party established the People's Republic of China on the continent, while the Nationalist Party regime fled to Taiwan. Both claimed to be the legitimate government of China.

In 1952, during the Cold War, Japan recognized the Nationalist Party regime in Taiwan as the legitimate government of China and signed a peace treaty. However, in 1972, the Japan-China Joint Communiqué established diplomatic relations between the People's Republic and Japan and resulted in Japan breaking off relations with Taiwan. In 1978, the Treaty of Peace and Friendship between Japan and China was concluded and Japan-China relations developed with a focus on economic issues. With the help of Japanese ODA, China achieved rapid economic development, Japanese firms invested in the country, and China became Japan's largest trading partner.

In the 21st century, China's GDP has exceeded Japan's becoming the second largest in the world, and China has an increasingly international presence. Between the two countries, there are historical issues relating to the war, as well problems related to the Senkaku islands that remain unresolved. However, Japan-China relations form an important bilateral relationship that influences not only China and Japan themselves, but the whole world. Both countries need to be aware of this fact and conduct diplomatic relations in a manner while thinking about the future of the world.

Japan-South Korea Relations

In 1910, in accordance with the Japan-Korea Treaty, Japan made Korea (Korean Empire) a colony. Japan's governance of Korea continued until Japan lost in the Second World War in 1945. In 1948, under the influence of the Cold War, the socialist Democratic People's Republic of Korea (North Korea) was established in the northern part of the Korean peninsula, and the liberal Republic of Korea was established in the south. In 1950, the Korean War broke out between the two countries (a

が始まりました（1953年休戦）。

日韓の国交正常化交渉は、植民地支配をめぐる認識の違いなどにより、なかなか進展しませんでした。1965年にようやく外交関係の樹立などを定めた日韓基本条約や、日本が韓国に対して行う経済協力に関する協定などが結ばれ、国交が正常化しました。

2002年には日韓共催のサッカーワールドカップが開かれ、その後、日本で韓流ドラマやK-POPなどが流行し、韓流ブームと呼ばれる現象も起きました。しかし、植民地支配に関わる歴史問題や竹島（韓国名「独島」）をめぐる問題が、日韓関係に影を落としています。隣国同士は、関係が密接である分、友好も対立も深くなる傾向があります。歴史を忘れることなく、未来志向の関係を築くためには、相手の立場になって考える姿勢が重要です。

【日露】

第二次世界大戦末期の1945年8月、ソビエト社会主義共和国連邦（ソ連）は、日ソ中立条約を破棄し、対日参戦しました。その際に北方四島（択捉島、国後島、色丹島および歯舞群島）も占領します。1956年、日本は日ソ共同宣言によりソ連と国交を回復します。ソ連は日本の国連加盟を支持するようになり、日本の国連加盟が実現しました。

その後、社会主義体制が崩壊し、ソ連は消滅、1991年にロシア連邦となりました。北方領土問題が解決していないために、日本はロシアと平和条約を結べていません。現在日露間で、北方領土における共同経済活動や、元島民の訪問の円滑化など、平和条約締結へ向けた努力が進められています。（土田宏成）

元島民による択捉島（ポンヤリ墓地）での墓参り（写真提供：独立行政法人北方領土問題対策協会）

ceasefire was established in 1953).

The normalization of diplomatic relations between Japan and South Korea did not progress smoothly due to differences in perception regarding Japan's colonial rule. Relations were finally normalized when the Treaty on Basic Relations between Japan and the Republic of Korea was signed in 1965 and agreements on economic cooperation were made.

In 2002, Japan and South Korea jointly held the FIFA World Cup and, following this, Korean Wave (Hallyu) TV dramas and K-POP artists became popular in Japan creating a Korean Wave boom in the country. However, historical issues relating to Japan's colonial rule over the Korean peninsula, and problems concerning the Liancourt Rocks (Takeshima in Japanese, Dokdo in Korean), cast a shadow over Japan-South Korea relations. As neighboring countries that are closely related to one another, both friendship and conflict between the two countries runs deep. Thinking from the position of the other party is important in order to build a future-orientated relationship without forgetting the past.

Japan-Russia Relations

Toward the end of World War II, in August 1945, the Union of Soviet Socialist Republics (Soviet Union) discarded the Soviet-Japanese Neutrality Pact and entered the war with Japan. At this time, the Soviet Union occupied the four islands of Iturup (Etorofu), Kunashir, Shikotan, and Habomai. In 1956, diplomatic relations between the Soviet Union and Japan recommenced with the Soviet-Japanese Joint Declaration. The Soviet Union supported Japan's bid to join the United Nations and Japan's accession to the United Nations came into effect.

The socialist regime of the Soviet Union collapsed and, in 1991, the country became the Russian Federation. The Northern Territories dispute has not been resolved so no peace treaty exists between Japan and Russia. Efforts are currently underway toward concluding a peace treaty including economic cooperation in the Northern Territories and the facilitation of former islanders visits. (Tr. M. Winchester)

❖日本の無形文化遺産❖

⓱ 結城紬
Yuki-tsumugi, silk fabric production technique

《絹織物の伝統的な製造技術》

　結城紬は常陸紬などともいわれ、古くより現在の茨城県結城市、栃木県小山市（旧絹村）を中心として製織されてきたものです。今なお、糸つむぎから機織りに至るまでのすべての工程において、手作業による伝統的な技法が守られ、良質のものが生産されています。織りには経糸を腰で吊ってその張り加減を調整する古式の織機を用います。

【登録年】2010年
【写　真】地機織り（提供：結城市教育委員会）

18 個人と家族
Individual and Family

【家族】

　日本の家族は「家」を形成する構造からなり、自立や独立を重んじる欧米の「核家族」とは違います。家は、家系を継承するために、一人の子が親の血筋を次の世代に繋げていくシステムです。家を継がない残りの兄弟姉妹たちは新しい家族を形成します。先祖から血筋を代々継承しているのが「本家」で、後者のうち生家と同じ姓を名乗る新しい家族が「分家」です。本家と分家の関係は継続して保たれ、本家を中心とする親族組織が形成されます。

　日本の家族は、家筋を継承することに誇りを持ち、敬意や感謝の念も共有します。この家族組織の「ウチ」の価値観は、家から出た外部の領域である「ソト」においても多様な社会組織の中に形成されます。同じ集団に所属する成員同士が「ウチ」の感覚を持ち、年齢や世代などの上下関係を重んじつつ親密な関係が形成されます。例えば職場や、学校教育の場や部活動の仲間で、この家族的な感情が共有されます。

【既婚／未婚】

　日本で既婚女性は、主に家事を担い家族を育む主婦像として自己肯定感を持ちます。他方、未婚女性は、自律して仕事に自らを見出し会社に貢献し自己実現のライフスタイルを追求している意識を持ちます。未婚女性は、既婚女性と比較すると、豊かな消費生活を満喫しながら、会社の中で「活躍」する女性というイメージがあるようです。

　しかし、「他律」と「自律」とで対比し、前者には「家族のため」という暗黙の美徳がある一方、後者の生

The Family

Japanese families are structured to form 'houses' (*ie*), which are different from European and American-style 'nuclear families' that emphasize a sense of independence. A 'house' is a system in which one child connects the parent's bloodline to the next generation in order to inherit the family tree. The remaining siblings who do not inherit the 'house' form new families. The family that inherits bloodlines from their ancestors are known as the 'head family' (*honke*) and the new families as 'branch families' (*bunke*) who take the same family name as the original house. The relationship between the 'head family' and the 'branch families' are maintained continuously and relations between relatives are formed with the 'head family' at the center.

Japanese families pride themselves on the inheritance of such family lines and share respect and admiration for them. The Japanese value of the 'interior' (*uchi*) is formed through diverse social organization and through its relationship with the 'exterior' (*soto*) realm outside the 'house' system. Members belonging to the same group have a sense of *uchi* and intimate relationships are formed that also respect hierarchical relationships such as age and generation. For example, this familial emotion is shared in the workplace, at school, and in club activities.

Married/Unmarried

Married women in Japan generally have a positive self-image of housewives who are in charge of housework and bringing up their families. On the other hand, unmarried women see themselves as pursuing lifestyles of self-actualization and contributing work independently to their company. There is an image of unmarried women, when compared to married women, as enjoying a rich consumer lifestyle and being highly valued in their companies for being 'active'.

However, when contrasted in terms of being 'heteronomous' and 'independent' forms of behavior, the former is praised for the implicit virtue of being 'for the family', and the latter way of living is thought to be 'for oneself' or 'for money.' Public opinion

き方は「自分のため」「お金のため」という評価もされます。世間からは他律的な生き方をする母親像が比較的高く評価されてきているのに対し、後者の独身の自律した女性は肩身の狭い思いをすることが少なくないのが現状です。背後にあるのは、恋愛感情を育み結婚して、新しい命を育み、次世代に自らを継承させることを高く評価する価値観があります。既婚女性は、他者への思い遣りや気配りを示し、家族を育むことが、「かけがえのない」ことだと感じることができます。

【育児】

　新しい命を育むことに関わる仕事全般、躾、教育等の役割を果す「母業」が美徳とされます。「働く母親」という言葉には、この母親像も投影されています。仕事を持つ母親たちは、賃金労働と共に家事労働という「二重負担」を背負っており、「良き母像」が逆に、母たちに精神的負担を与えてもいます。

　子育てが楽しいかどうかの調査では、半数のみが賛同しているにすぎず、現実には不安やストレスを持つ母親たちも多いです。子どもが3歳までは母親が家で育てるべきという「神話」もあり、あえて育児を犠牲にし、子どもを施設に預けて仕事を優先することに抵抗感を抱く母親たちも多いです。育児分担では、8割が母親、2割が父親で、夫は育児に「協力する」という形でのみ関わり、育休制度を活用する男性は3％程度に留まります。実際に、子育てに参加する父である「イクメン」はごく少数です。子どもを預けられる保育施設も圧倒的に少なく、「働く母親」のニーズにあっていないのが現状です。　（吉田光宏）

regards the image of a mother who lives for others highly, while single people who live for themselves are often viewed as thinking very narrowly. Behind this opinion lies a value system that highly values the notion that people marry after falling in love and create new life passing on to the next generation. Married women can express feelings of concern and be attentive to others and feel that nurturing a family is something 'irreplaceable.'

Childcare

All work that concerns the nurturing of new life, including that which fulfills the role of discipline and education, is considered as part of the virtue of 'maternity.' This image of the mother is imbued in words like 'the working mother.' Mothers who work carry the 'double burden' of wage labor and domestic labor and 'good mother' images consequently provide them with psychological burden.

In a survey asking whether parenting is fun, only half agree and there are many mothers who are stressed and experience anxiety. Myths that say mothers should nurture their children at home until the age of 3 also exist and there are many mothers who resist placing work as a priority over child care, sacrificing carrying out child care themselves and leaving their children in care facilities. The percentage of childcare responsibility among parents in Japan stands at 80% for mothers and 20% for fathers. Husbands are often involved only in 'cooperating' with child rearing and men using the childcare leave system in Japan stands at around only 3%. So-called *ikumen* who take part in childcare are overwhelmingly small in number. There is a shortage of childcare facilities in Japan and the needs of 'working mothers' are far from being met. (Tr. M. Winchester)

【一人前】

　「一人前」になるとは、「自由な雰囲気」や「誰にも邪魔されない感覚」を満喫した後に、「社会」に出て「新たな世界」で認められる自律した状態になることを指します。「一人前」の社会的評価を獲得するのに大切なのは、「苦労」していくことだと認識されます。また、仕事を通じて多様な人たちの役に立ち、貢献していく中で評価されていきます。仕事で自律するための知識や技能を身につける一方で、多くの困難や問題に向き合い適切に対処していくことも期待されます。目上の人たちの知見を吸収し、自らを修練し人格が形成されてはじめて一人前とみなされます。

　また、一人前になることは社会の中で、世間の基準を満たす「人」としての評価を確立することを指します。「額に汗して働き」、複雑な人間関係の中を泳ぐ処世術も身につけていきます。多様な責務をこなす学びのプロセスで、心を磨き、高い精神性を育んだ末に到達される人格です。学校教育においても、一人前になるための基礎的な土台を学んでいます。

【引きこもり】

　学校や仕事に行く立場でありながら、自己肯定感を持てず、自分の状態を恥じ、家にこもり、社会とのコミュニケーションをとらない子どもや若者が増えています。過分に干渉する母親と仕事人間で家庭に無関心な父親との間で、期待に応えようとする「良い子」に引きこもる傾向があると言われています。

　引きこもりは、子の成長期の多感な思いと、家族からの期待や躾などとの関係が上手く噛みあわず、

Ichininmae

Becoming *ichininmae* means entering a state of autonomy in which you are recognized by the 'new world' to which you enter when you become a part of society after a period in which you have enjoyed a sense of 'free atmosphere' in which you 'are not disturbed by anybody.' In order to be evaluated socially as *ichininmae*, 'struggle' is thought of as important. Helping all sorts of people through your work and contributing to society is also highly regarded. While acquiring knowledge and skills to ensure your autonomy, you are also expected to cope with many difficulties and problems and deal with them appropriately. You are regarded as *ichininmae* only after absorbing the knowledge of superiors and forming your own personality through training.

In addition, becoming *ichininmae* means putting yourself in society and establishing an evaluation of yourself as someone who meets public standards. Through 'working with sweat on your forehead' you will acquire the means to negotiate complex human relationships. The character of someone who is *ichininmae* is that which is reached at the end of a process of learning to fulfill your various obligations, refining your mind, and fostering a high sense of spirit. Even in school education, people are learning the basic foundations they will need to become *ichininmae*.

Hikikomori

Young people who, despite reaching an age in which they would usually be expected to be in education or find work, often fail to gain a sense of self-worth, are ashamed of their predicament, and retreat inside the home avoiding communication with the rest of society, are on the rise. It is thought that this is due to a tendency for so-called 'good children' to try to answer the hopes invested in them by overprotective mothers and fathers who are 'workaholics' and indifferent to their families.

Hikikomori, or young people who withdraw from society, are produced when the diverse feelings that children have when

それにより個人と社会との接点が外れることで、生み出されると言われています。自分の能力や人格を認められていくことで得られる自己肯定感を持つことができず、家族からも、また否定的に見られていると思い込み、社会にも溶け込めず悩んでいきます。

鬱や人格障害などが出て、場合によっては社会への恨みを持つ人もいます。親から愛されたにもかかわらず「自分をきちんと育てられなかった親が悪い」という被害妄想から、否定的な自己像を持ってしまい、反社会的な考えを持つこともあります。

【フリーター】

フリーターとは、卒業後、「自分探し」のために敢えて定職に就くのではなく、自由に好きなことを探し「夢を実現する」ことに価値を見出し、会社の正社員にならずに所属意識を持たない人たちです。主婦を除くアルバイト、パート、派遣労働者および、働く意志がありながら無職の人たちなどを指します。

中には、実際に自分の夢の実現に向けて努力をして技能を身に付けていく高い意識を持つ人たちもいます。正規雇用を希望しても、実際にはその希望が適わなかった人たちもいます。2020年では、若年層（15～34歳）のフリーターは約136万人です。

社会的に不安定な状況にある人たちも多く、時に過重労働を強いられたり、社会に居場所を感じられずにストレスを過剰に抱えている人たちも出ています。社会との繋がりを実感できない場合、他者からの承認も得られず、自分に対して否定的になる傾向もあります。このため、自責や屈辱の念にかられ、自傷行為に及ぶ人たちもいます。

（吉田光宏）

they are growing up do not sit well with the expectations and discipline offered to them by their families. It is said that, because of this, point of contact between the individual and society is removed. These children cannot gain a sense of self-worth usually obtained through recognition of their character and abilities. They therefore come to believe that they are being denied by their families and worry that they cannot immerse themselves in society.

Some examples of the psychological symptoms they face include depression, personality disorder, and in some cases, people develop a grudge against society itself. Despite the fact that they were loved by their parents, these people develop a 'victim complex' through which they think 'it was the fault of parents who did not raise me properly' and through this negative self-image they come to possess anti-social ideas.

Furītā

Furītā are people who instead of taking a regular job after graduation choose to 'search for themselves', see value in 'realizing their dreams' and do not become regular full-time employees. They include part-time and temporary workers, excluding housewives, and unemployed people who are willing to work.

Some *Furītā* actively try to develop skills in order to strive toward the realization of their dreams. Even when people desire to enter regular employment, there are people who are unable to achieve this goal. In 2020, the number of young people (15 to 34 years olds) working as *Furītā* was 1,360,000.

There are many people who find themselves in precarious social circumstances, and people have also emerged who are unable to find a place for themselves in society. As a result of this, they experience extreme levels of stress. There is a tendency that people become negative about themselves when they are unable to gain the recognition of others and do not feel a connection with society. For this reason, some people are caught up in self-reproach and humiliation which can also lead to self-harm. (Tr. M. Winchester)

日本人的対人コミュニケーションの根底にある日本文化

　日常生活で重んじられる対人関係では、言葉による意思疎通と同時に、当事者同士の感情や情緒を大切にしています。相手との関係形成で独立した自分を主張するというよりは、相手を信じて頼り、自分も相手の思いを受け止めようとするような、持ちつ持たれつの互恵関係を形成します。情緒的で包容力ある関係を前提とした以心伝心の理解をしていきます。言葉は必ずしも必要としない信頼関係で、相手に依存する「甘え」の感情が土台にあります。原初的には、母と子の関係にあり、相手を全面的に信頼し、頼られた者は情緒的に受け入れ、期待に応えようとします。

　この母性的感情による相互関係は、日常社会全体に持ち込まれ、相手の思いや立場を配慮していきながら、逐次適切な関係を把握し態度や行動に示していくことが期待されます。「自分」とは、この人と人との「間」や「繋がり」の中で形成されていく感覚です。そこで、相手の状況や心情を言葉で説明しなくても察知しあえる対人関係が形成されます。欧米社会では言葉を通じての相互理解が大前提で、相手との区別や対立も踏まえ自己の意思や要求を伝え合います。他方、日本の情緒に基づいたコミュニケーションでは、情報共有や意思伝達は、言葉を通じて論理的に説得していくような努力を伴わなくても十分に可能である場合も多いです。

　相手を「理解」しようとする時、言葉だけの説明で充足するとは必ずしも言えません。例えば「口先だけの人間」「言わぬが花」などの慣用表現のように、言葉の表現そのものよりは「腹を探る」「目は口ほどにものを言う」というように、言外の心中を把握しようとすることも重んじます。相互信頼関係が既に出来ている場合、「話さなくても分かる」ということも生じます。このように、日本では、感情中心型のコミュニケーションが根底にあります。　　（吉田光宏）

The Japanese Culture at the Root of Japanese Style Communication

In the interpersonal relationships we value in our daily lives, the feelings and affects of the communicating parties are regarded as just as important as communication through words. Rather than asserting one's individual self, we form a reciprocal relationship through trusting and relying upon that other person and making efforts to accept their thoughts and ideas. Through relationships of affective tolerance, we gain a tacit understanding of others. The feeling of *amae* (dependency) and sense of relying on the other person is located at the base of relationships of trust that do not necessarily rely upon words.

It is considered desirable that reciprocal relationships based upon maternal emotions such as *amae* can be brought into relationships across the whole of everyday society. People's sense of 'self' is an emotion that is formed in the 'ties' made 'between' themselves and others. Therefore, interpersonal relationships can be formed based upon perceptions of the situation or feelings of others without explanation. In European and North American society, mutual understanding based upon words is a major premise. Intentions and demands are communicated taking into account the distinctions and points of potential conflict between people. In contrast, in communication based on Japanese emotions, the sharing of information and communication of people's intentions can be sufficiently achieved without efforts to convince one's interlocutor through logical words.

When trying to 'understand' one's interlocutor, it is not necessarily true that you will be satisfied with explanations that rely only upon words. For example, as in the idiomatic expressions *kuchi dake no ningen* ('a person who is all talk') or *iwanu ga hana* ('the less said about it the better'), efforts to grasp non-verbal affects such as *hara wo saguru* (lit. 'probing the belly') or *me wa kuchi hodo ni mono wo iu* ('the eyes say as much as the mouth') are valued just as much in Japanese society. When mutual relationships of trust have been achieved, people are able to 'understand one another without speaking.' Thus, in Japan, emotional-centered communication is fundamental.

(Tr. M. Winchester)

❖日本の無形文化遺産❖

⑱ 壬生の花田植

Mibu no Hana Taue, ritual of transplanting rice in Mibu, Hiroshima

《広島県壬生の田植えの儀式》

●

　広島県北広島町で行われている農耕儀礼で、稲作の無事と豊作を祈願し、特定の田を儀礼の場とし、田の神を迎えて盛大に田植えを行います。美しい鞍や艶やかな飾りをつけた飾り牛が一列になり代掻きをし、サンバイと呼ばれる人たちがササラと呼ばれる打楽器を打ち鳴らしながら田植唄を歌って指揮をとります。その音頭にあわせ、絣の着物を着た早乙女が横一列に並び苗を植えていきます。

●

【登録年】2011年
【写　真】早乙女（提供：北広島町役場）

⟨19⟩ 教育の諸相

Aspects of Education

【いじめ】

　いじめとは、自分より弱い者に対して、暴力やいやがらせを加え、身体的・心理的に苦痛を与えることです。1980年代、校内暴力が沈静化するとともに、いじめが原因とみられる不登校、自殺、事件が多発し、90年代になって深刻な社会問題、政治問題となり、現在に至っています。

　政府は2013年に、「いじめ防止対策推進法」を制定するなど、対応を続けています。しかし、2020年度の小・中・高等学校及び特別支援学校における、いじめの認知件数は61万2496件と、前年度より6万8563件増加しており、調査を開始した1985年度以降、最高となっています。

　近年は、パソコンや携帯電話を使用したインターネット上で、誹謗中傷する「ネットいじめ」が急増しています。無断で相手の個人情報をさらしたり、裏サイトなどでの誹謗中傷を繰り返したり、なりすまし投稿をするといった行為です。その実態把握と解決に向けた取り組みは、大きな課題となりました。

【教育格差】

　教育格差とは、生まれ育った環境により受けることのできる教育に、格差が生じることです。その最大の要因は親の収入の多寡であり、その経済格差によって、受けられる教育に大きな違いが生じます。

　文部科学省の「2019年度子供の学習費調査」によると、家庭が負担する教育支出のうち、学校外教育費（塾費等）が公立高校で約18万、私立高校で約29万円となっています。2017年度の全国学力テストの結果

Bullying

Bullying (*ijime* in Japanese) refers to the act of physically and psychologically abusing others who are perceived as being weaker, through violence and harassment. Beginning with the 1980s, even as in-school violence became less prominent, there was a surge in cases of absenteeism, suicide, and various other incidents in which the cause was *ijime*, to such an extent that in the 1990s it became a serious social and political problem, and it continues to be today.

The government is constantly trying to find solutions by adopting various measures such as the Bullying Prevention Law from 2013. Despite this, the number of bullying-related incidents in elementary, middle, high and special schools in 2020 was of 612,496, an increase of 68,563 compared to the previous year. This was also the highest figure recorded since statistics started to be compiled in 1985.

In recent years, there has also been a surge in cases of cyber-bullying, in which intimidation and threats are made on the internet by using computers or mobile phones. Cyber-bullying involves acts such as exposing somebody's personal information without their permission, making repeated threats on various sites, and stealing somebody else's identity. Grasping the extent of these incidents and adopting countermeasures is an urgent task.

Educational inequality

Educational inequality refers to the inequality in chances to have access to education due to the environment in which a person is born and raised. The main cause is the income of the parents, as economic disparities lead to disparities in the access to education.

According to the report on the cost of education for children published by the MEXT in 2019, fees for extracurricular educational activities which are borne by the family — such as tuition fees for cram schools — can go as high as 180,000 yen in the case of public high schools, and 290,000 yen in the case of private high schools. Results of the 2017 national test of scholastic performance show that there is a large gap in the

では、世帯収入の多寡で学力テストの正答率に大きな開きがありました。世帯収入が低い家庭の子どもほど、学力テストの正答率が低いことが示されました。

　つまり、高収入の親の許に生まれた子どもは、大学への進学実績が高い私立校に通い、ハイレベルな塾や予備校にも通うことができるのです。結果として、有名難関大学に入学しています。

　日本においては、最終学歴がその人の人生を左右することが、比較的大きいと言われています。そのため、教育格差は世代を超えた格差の固定化につながるとの危険性が指摘され、社会問題化しています。

【入学試験】

　入学試験とは、一般的には高校・大学が入学志願者の中から合格者を選別するために実施するものです。近年は、私立の小学校や中学校の入学試験にも多数の志願者が集まり、注目を集めています。

　2021年度学校基本調査によると、大学・短大進学率（過年度卒含む）は58.9％と過去最高を記録し、今や大学入試は一般的なものとなっています。

　大学入試の多様化が進んでいる現在では、推薦入試やAO入試の導入だけでなく、一般入試も大学によって形態が様々です。また、共通入学試験「大学入試センター試験」の存在は、大きな特色です。毎年1月中旬に全国で一斉に実施され、例年50万人以上が受験する日本最大規模の試験です。

　しかし、全問、マークシートで解答するため、知識偏重型との批判があります。そのため、2020年度からは、思考力・判断力・表現力を問う「大学入学共通テスト」が実施される予定です。　　（町田明広）

proportion of correct answers between high-income and low-income family students. This indicates that the lower the family income, the lower the percentage of correct answers.

In other words, children whose parents have a high income have the opportunity to go to private schools that are far better than public schools when it comes to the number of students who go to university after graduation, and they can go to high-level preparatory and cram schools. This allows them to enter famous universities which are higly selective.

It is often said that in Japan a person's academic background influences their life to a great extent. There are voices that point out that, as a consequence, there is the danger that educational inequality might create a spiral of inequality that spans over more than one generation, and that it is a serious social problem.

Entrance examination

Entrance examinations are held by high schools and universities in order to select successful candidates from among all the applicants. In recent years, there has been an increase in the number of applicants for private elementary and middle schools, a matter that has attracted a lot of attention.

According to a 2021 survey of the education system, the rate of enrollment in universities and colleges (including high school graduates from previous years) was 58.9%, the highest on record. This suggests that the entrance examination has become a normal thing for most people.

Nowadays, there is a diversification of entrance examinations, and there are many differences between universities, as some prefer to select students based on recommendations or on a portfolio, while other organize their own examination. One of the peculiarities of the system in Japan is the existence of the so-called "Central Examination," a national exam the results of which can be used by all universities. It is held in January all across the country and it is the biggest examination in Japan, with over 500,000 applicants taking it every year.

However, the examination is often criticized for focusing on rote memorization, as all questions have to be answered on mark sheets. A new type of exam called "The Common University Entrance Examination," which emphasizes critical thinking and the students' ability to think and to express themselves, is scheduled to start in 2020. (Tr. R. Pașca)

19 | 教育の諸相

形

『諳厄利亜語林大成』
(長崎歴史文化博物館所蔵)

『諳厄利亜語林大成』
(長崎歴史文化博物館所蔵)

【英語教育】

　日本初の英和辞典は、1808年に長崎港で起きたフェートン号事件を受けてイギリス研究の必要性を意識した幕府が、オランダ語通詞らに編纂させた『諳厄利亜語林大成』でした。その後、明治の近代的な学校制度で外国語としての英語が導入され、本格的な英語教育が始まります。

　現在、グローバル化が進む中で日本企業の海外進出も急速化し、生徒や学生のみならず社会人の英語能力も求められています。就職試験時に英語テストのスコアを採用判断の基準にする企業も多くなり、教育機関でも英語力向上のために様々な取り組みが始まっています。2011年度から小学校5・6年で必修化された英語に親しむための「外国語活動」も、その開始が2020年度からは3年に早められ、5年と6年では教科書を使う正式な「外国語科」の履修が始まります。

　しかし、教科書の制作や教授法の獲得など、教材や教員養成に関する課題が数多く残っています。

【ゆとり教育】

　ゆとり教育は1980年度に施行された学習指導要領から始まったとされ、具体的に実施されたのは2002年度以降です。その趣旨は、詰め込み型の教育方針を是正し、思考力や批判力を鍛錬する学習を重視し、ゆとりのある学校を目指すことでした。

　ゆとり教育の最終的な目的は、知識を暗記することへの偏重から脱却し、創造力や柔軟性に重きを置き、学習時間と内容を減らしながら「生きる力」を育

English language education

The first English-Japanese dictionary was the *Angeria Gorin Taisei*, compiled in 1814 by Dutch interpreters under orders from the bakufu, which had become aware of the necessity to study English following the Nagasaki Harbor Incident of 1808. Later, with the modernization of the education system during the Meiji period, English was introduced in schools as a subject of study. This represents the beginning of English language education in Japan.

At present, in the age of globalization, as more Japanese companies are rapidly expanding abroad, good English language skills have become a requirement not only for students, but for business persons as well. There is an increasing number of companies that use English test scores as a criterion when they hire new employees, and educational institutions are implementing various strategies to improve the English level of their students. "Foreign language activities" became a compulsory subject for 5th and 6th grade elementary school students in 2011, with the purpose to familiarize them with the language. English was supposed to become a compulsory subject in 2020, but the date was moved up by three years and now 5th and 6th grade students study English formally.

However, there still remain many problems that need to be solved, such as the production of textbooks and training programs for teachers.

Yutori education

Yutori education ("no-pressure education") is considered to have begun with the introduction of a new course of study in 1980, but it was officially implemented after 2002. Its main purpose was to shift focus from preparing students for standardized testing to a student-centered approach with an emphasis on developing critical thinking abilities — in other words, to create "no-pressure" schools.

The goal of *yutori* education was to break away from the emphasis on rote learning and to nurture the students' "ability to live" by cultivating their creativity and flexibility while at the same time reducing the number of hours spent at school and the

むこととされていました。その一環として「学校週5日制」が導入され、「総合的な学習の時間」などの新科目が設置されました。

　ゆとり教育に対する見解は、学力の低下につながったと批判する声もある一方、学力はテストの結果だけでは測りきれないと指摘する専門家もいるなど、賛否両論があります。そんな中で、2011年度の学習指導要領の改訂に伴って学習量の増加傾向が進み、この新しい教育理念はマスコミなどで「脱ゆとり教育」と呼ばれています。

【日本の大学】

　大学の役割は、理論や実践を学ぶための場を提供し、将来的に社会や国を担うエリートを養成することだと言われています。文部科学省の2021年のデータによると日本における大学・短大進学率は58.9%で、先進国の中でも極めて高い数字です。また、東京大学が世界大学ランキングベスト40に入るなど、日本における高等教育の質も高く評価されています。

　日本の大学のほとんどが入試センター試験を採用しています。しかし、解答をマークシートに記入する方式であることが批判され、最近、記述式の設問を導入している大学も増えています。

　ここ数十年、少子化が深刻化し日本の大学も学生の減少という問題に直面しています。その対策としてクォーター制を導入したり、英語で学位が取れるプログラムを新設したりなど、留学生の受け入れに積極的に取り組んでいる大学が増加しつつあります。

（ロマン・パシュカ）

content of the curriculum. The "five-day school week" was put in place, and new subjects such as "General learning" were introduced.

Opinions on *yutori* education are divided: on the one hand, there are voices that criticize it by claiming that it leads to a decline in the students' academic ability, and on the other hand there are specialists who point out that academic ability cannot be measured by standardized testing alone. In 2011, changes in the course of study brought back the tendency to increase the number of study hours for students. The media call this new education policy *datsu yutori* ("post-no-pressure") education.

Japanese universities

It is often said that the role of the university is to provide a place where one can learn both theory and practice, and to train the elites who will be the leaders of the future. According to MEXT statistics from 2021, the rate of enrollment in universities and colleges in Japan is 58.9%, an extremely high proportion among developed countries. Japanese higher education institutions are appreciated for the quality of the education they provide, with the University of Tokyo, for example, constantly ranking among the top 40 in the world.

Most Japanese universities use the results of a national, centralized test to select students. This system has been criticized because it only consists of multiple choice questions to be answered on mark sheets, and recently there has been an increase in the number of universities that organize their own examination with a focus on essay writing.

Over the last decades, the declining birthrate has become a serious issue and Japanese universities are now facing the problem of a constantly decreasing number of students. As a countermeasure, many universities have become more active in trying to attract foreign students by switching from a semester system to a quarter one and by founding new programs in which students can get their degree in English. (R. Paşca)

教育の昔・今・これから

　日本における最古の教育機関は栃木県にある足利学校であると言われ、鎌倉時代に創設されたとの説があります。江戸時代になると、寺院で師匠が町人の子どもに読み書きや計算などを教える施設が発展していきます。当時の生徒は「寺子」と呼ばれ、複数の寺子が一人の師匠に教えてもらう制度でした。

　明治時代に入ると、福沢諭吉など、学者の影響により近代思想が普及し、教育制度が確立されます。1871年に設置された文部省は、欧米の科学や技術の導入に熱心で、日本人学生の留学を促したり「お雇い外国人」を招いたりすることで教育の質を高めようと努力しました。その結果、短期間で日本も世界的水準の研究成果を発表できるようになりました。

　戦後、自由主義思想が導入され、教育の機会均等と男女平等が原則とされました。現在、日本の教育制度は高く評価され、例えば経済協力開発機構（OECD）が実施する「学習到達度調査（PISA）」では、数学的リテラシーや読解力など、ほぼ全てのカテゴリーでベスト10に入ります。

　しかし、一方で課題も多く残っています。近年、長期不登校、いじめ、体罰など、生徒が日々直面している問題が深刻化し、その解決策は急務であると言えます。教師も、授業の他に部活動の顧問も任せられることもあり、多忙になり、過労死のケースも報告されています。また、研究活動においても、研究成果のほとんどが日本語のみで発表されることによって国際化が遅れており、日本の大学の「ガラパゴス化」も指摘されています。

　これらの問題について議論し、どのようにして乗り越えていけるのかということについて、検討することがこれからの社会全体としての課題であり、チャレンジでもあります。　　（ロマン・パシュカ）

The past, present and future of education

The oldest educational institution in Japan is said to be the Ashikaga school located in Tochigi prefecture, which according to some theories was founded in the Kamakura period. The Edo period saw the development of facilities attached to temples, where a master would teach the children of the *chōnin* reading, writing and calculus. At the time, students were called "terako." Several students learned all the subjects from one master.

In the Meiji period, due to the influence of thinkers like Yukichi Fukuzawa, a modern education system was established. The Ministry of Education was founded in 1871 and it focused on the adoption of Western science and technology, striving to raise the level of education in Japan by encouraging Japanese students to go and study abroad and by hiring foreigners to work in Japan.

After World War II, with the introduction of liberalism, equal access to education and gender equality became fundamental principles. At present, the Japanese education system is highly regarded, and Japan is ranked among the top 10 countries in all categories of the PISA scholastic performance study conducted by the OECD.

However, there are still many issues that need to be addressed. In recent years, problems that students are confronted with on a daily basis such as bullying, long-term absenteeism, or corporal punishment have become very serious, and solutions are urgently needed. Teachers are often overworked because in addition to their classes they also have to coordinate extra-curricular activities such as student clubs, and there have even been reports of *karōshi* cases. As for research, there are voices that talk about a "Galápagos syndrome" of Japanese universities, pointing out a failure to internationalize because most of the research results are published only in Japanese.

Engaging in a debate about all these problems and trying to find a solution to overcome them will represent both a task and a challenge for society as a whole. (Tr. R. Paşca)

❖日本の無形文化遺産❖

⓳ 那智の田楽

Nachi no Dengaku, a religious performing art held at the Nachi fire festival

《那智の「火祭り」で奉納される舞台芸能》

　「那智の田楽」は14-15世紀、京都の田楽法師が伝えたとされる芸能で、和歌山県にある熊野那智大社の扇祭（通称：火祭り）で毎年7月14日、国土安泰や豊作を祈って奉納されます。笛の音に合わせて「ビンザラ」「締太鼓」など、楽器を鳴らしながら様々に陣形を変えて踊ります。「那智の田楽」の後に「火祭り」が始まると、那智大社の例大祭はクライマックスを迎えます。

【登録年】2012年
【写　真】那智の田楽（提供：和歌山県）

現代社会の課題

Challenges for Contemporary Society

【終身雇用制】

終身雇用制は、戦後に大企業を中心に一般化した雇用制度です。海外では日本古来の伝統と言われることが多いですが、労使間の緊張やストライキを抑えるため、会社への忠誠と献身と引き換えに生涯雇用を約束するという方針のもとに導入された制度で、日本の労働者すべてに当てはまるものではありません。

この制度では、会社側は卒業直後の学生を新卒として採用し、研修を受けさせます。不況の際でも解雇されないという安心感は会社への忠誠心や勤務態度の向上につながります。出世はおおむね年功序列です。そのため才能があっても転職は難しく、会社への献身度合や気風への迎合が重視され、改革や創意工夫はあまり歓迎されません。1990年代後半から2000年代前半の長引く不況によって様々な弱点が明らかになり、終身雇用制は徐々に崩れていっています。しかし、現在増加している派遣や契約労働制度は安定性がなく、多くの問題を抱えています。

【過労死】

過労死とは、過剰な労働による精神的・肉体的疲労が原因で死亡することをいいます。この用語が使われるようになったのは1970年代からですが、過労死自体はその前から起こっています。毎日長時間（場合によっては残業手当なしで）働くことを当然とする社会的風潮と文句を言いづらい文化を背景に、従業員を食い物にする会社もあります。これらの会社は「ブラック企業」と呼ばれます。

普段から長時間労働をしている人の場合、心筋梗

Lifetime Employment System

The lifetime employment system was a defining characteristic of many large corporations during the postwar era. Although it was discussed even outside Japan as an old "tradition" in Japanese culture, this was untrue. It was in fact the result of specific policies intended to relieve labor tensions and strikes by giving workers secure employment in exchange for loyalty and a total commitment to their companies. It never characterized all workers in Japan.

Companies would recruit workers fresh out of school and invest in training them. Workers, secure that they would not be fired even during economic downturns, felt loyal to their companies and would work hard, being rewarded with promotions as they aged. However, the system made it difficult for even talented individuals to change jobs, and rewarded seniority over skill. Hard work and company spirit were valued over innovation and ingenuity.

The weaknesses of the system became more obvious during the prolonged recession of the 1990s and early 2000s, leading to its gradual collapse. The current system, characterized by many temporary or limited positions with little job security, has many problems of its own.

Death from Overwork

Karōshi is a Japanese word that refers to people dying from exhaustion or medical problems due to overwork. The term began to be used in the 1970s although the phenomenon itself is much older. The social expectation that employees will work long hours every day, including often excessive and unpaid overtime, combined with the cultural reluctance among employees to complain, makes it comparatively easy for companies to exploit workers. Particularly bad companies have been given the moniker "black companies."

Employees forced to work excessive hours on a regular basis have been shown to be at greater risk from heart attacks and strokes. There are also psychological risks because overwork,

塞や脳卒中のリスクが高まります。またプライベートや睡眠の不足は、うつ病や自殺の可能性を高めることが指摘されています。過剰労働による従業員の死や自殺に関して、雇用者である会社がどの程度責を負うべきなのかについては議論の的で、政府も個々の会社の従業員への待遇についてはあまり干渉しない姿勢を取っています。2000年代前半から、「過労死」は英語として認められるようになりました。

【公害】

工業公害は、日本の近代化・経済発展の過程で起こった大きな社会問題の1つです。

19世紀後半の栃木県の足尾銅山事件では、河川汚染をはじめ周囲の環境に著しいダメージを与え、その際の政府の対応の遅さに、大きな抗議行動が起こりました。同じような公害として熊本県の水俣病があります。数十年にわたって水銀汚染された魚を食した地域の人々は、体が不自由になったり、亡くなったりしました。世論の高まりによって法規制がなされたのは1970年代のことです。しかし、バブル経済の時代には多くの企業が環境破壊を続けました。

今日ではリサイクルやエコの概念が人々の間に広まり、高い水準の環境管理が政府にも工場にも求められるようになりました。しかし、いまだゴミの焼却処理により多量の二酸化炭素が排出され、原子力の安全・無公害な活用について模索が続いています。また粗大ごみの処理手数料を払いたくないために、森林などに不法投棄する人々も問題となっています。

（亀井ダイチ・アンドリュー）

leaving little time for social life or even sleep, is a leading cause of depression and greatly increases the risk of suicide. The extent to which a corporation can be legally held responsible for an employee's death or suicide due to overwork is a controversial issue, and while the government has taken some steps it has been reluctant to interfere too much with companies' treatment of their employees. Since the 2000s, the term *karōshi* has also entered English.

Pollution

Pollution, particularly industrial pollution produced by industries during modernization, has been a major issue in modern Japanese society.

In the late nineteenth century the Ashio copper mine in Tochigi Prefecture was responsible for severe environmental damage, especially ruining rivers. The government was slow to respond, prompting a storm of protest. A similar story played out later in Minamata, Kumamoto Prefecture, where a chemical manufacturer dumped mercury in the water for decades, resulting in consumption of contaminated fish by the locals, many of whom became sick or died. Public outrage finally prompted the government to pass pollution legislation during the 1970s, but during the bubble era many corporations continued to disregard the environment.

Today, Japanese citizens, used to recycling and "eco" products, demand a higher standard of environmental stewardship from both the government and companies. However, numerous problems remain. Japan incinerates the majority of its waste, generates large amounts of carbon dioxide, and struggles to deal with nuclear power in a safe and non-polluting manner. Individuals dumping large articles of rubbish in forests to avoid paying collection fees is also a worrying concern.

(A. T. Kamei-Dyche)

【少子化】

「少子高齢化」とは出産数の減少と老年人口の増大が同時に進んでいる現象であり、現在は日本のみならず多くの先進国が直面している深刻な社会問題の1つです。この少子高齢化の主な原因としては、未婚化や晩婚化、そしてそれらに伴う晩産化や無産化がよく挙げられます。その他に、子育てにかかる養育費や教育費などの費用の増大も考えられます。

厚生労働省などのデータによると、日本では2005年に出生数が110万を切りましたが、減少の傾向は現在も続いています。少子化の一番大きな影響としては、労働人口の減少による国の成長力の低迷だと言われています。

少子化対策には、最近よくマスコミでも取り上げられているように保育施設の整備、育児休暇制度の拡充、共働き夫婦支援制度、そして出産後の再就職へのサポートなどがあります。

【限界集落】

近年、少子高齢化が進行している結果、「限界集落」という用語もメディアなどでしばしば耳にするようになりました。人口の5割以上が65歳以上の高齢者になった村や町では冠婚葬祭など、そのコミュニティの共同生活に必要不可欠な行事の維持が難しくなり、社会的に限界に近いことから「限界集落」と呼ばれるようになりました。

特に離島や中山間地域に多い限界集落は、若い人たちが就職のために都市部へ流出したり、学校や医療機関が統廃合、または閉鎖されたり、農業などの

Low Birthrate

The combination of a diminishing number of children and an aging population is a serious social problem that currently plagues many developed countries, including Japan. One of the main causes of this phenomenon is the recent tendency for people to marry later or stay single, which causes a decrease in the total number of children being born. Other causes include the increasing costs of child rearing and tuition fees for education.

According to official data of the Ministry of Health, Labor and Welfare of Japan, 2005 was the first year when the number of births dropped below the 1,100,000 figure, and the decreasing tendency continues in the present. It is said that the most important consequence of the low birthrate will be a negative influence on the work force, thus affecting the country's potential for growth.

As the media have been reporting recently, among the measures meant to counter the low birthrate are the construction of new facilities for children, parental leave expansion, a support system for couples where both spouses work, and support for women to return to the workplace after childbirth.

Marginal Villages

In recent years, as a result of the low birthrate and of the rapidly aging population, "marginal villages" (*genkai shūraku*) has become a term often used in media reports. A "marginal village" is a community close to its social limits, where more than 50% of the population consists of elderly people over 65 and where it has become difficult to hold various ceremonies and rituals —— such as marriages and funerals —— that are indispensable for coexistence within the community.

Most of the marginal villages are isolated on remote islands or in mountainous areas. This is a very serious problem that Japanese society is facing, because in these areas young people migrate to the city in search of employment, schools and health care institutions are merged or even closed down, and there is an acute shortage of labor for agriculture and industry.

産業の担い手がいなくなったりするなど、現在日本が抱えているかなり深刻な社会問題です。

2010年に実施された総務省の調査によると、限界集落は日本全国で約1万か所あり、これは調査対象となった集落のうちの15.5%を占めています。さらに、ここ数年、このような限界に近い集落の例は、東京都など都市部でも見られるようになりました。

【地域再生】

限界集落の広がりに歯止めをかけようと、ここ数年各地方で地域活性化(いわゆる「まちおこし」)をめざして試行錯誤しながら様々な取り組みが行われています。例えば、空き家や古民家を解体せずに改修し、カフェやレストラン、または宿泊施設に変えたり、あるいは耕作放棄地を農場化したりするなど、その地域に活気を取り戻すための試みが多くなってきています。

「まちおこし」には、既存の建築物の再生や交通手段の整備といったハード面と、その地域の歴史や文化の再発見や再評価といったソフト面の、2つの側面があります。

このような活動の課題としては、例えば、長期に渡って閉店が続く「シャッター街」の活性化、家屋の劣化対策、高齢者や障害者への配慮、空き地の有効利用などが挙げられます。「まちおこし」事業を成功に導くためには、その地域に住んでいる人たちの「協働」が必要不可欠だと言われています。

(ロマン・パシュカ)

A 2010 survey conducted by the Ministry of Internal Affairs found that there were approximately 10,000 marginal villages across Japan, which represents 15.5% of the total number of communities surveyed. Moreover, in the past few years, such marginal communities have also been found in big metropolises like Tokyo.

Regional Revitalization

Recently, in an attempt to put a stop to the spread of marginal communities, numerous projects of "regional revitalization" (*machi okoshi*) have been started in various areas across Japan, in a trial and error process. Such projects involve, for example, preserving old and abandoned houses and transforming them into cafes, restaurants and accommodation facilities, or turning abandoned plots into arable land with the purpose of bringing back vitality to the area.

Regional revitalization projects have two sides: a "hard" side which involves preservation of old buildings or construction of new roads, and a "soft" side which refers to the rediscovery and reevaluation of the cultural and historical heritage of the region.

Such projects have to deal with many challenges, like the revitalization of the so-called "shutter streets" that are lined with closed-down shops or offices, the deterioration of houses, accessibility for the elderly and for people with disabilities, and an efficient use of empty plots. For a revitalization project to become successful, the cooperation of the local residents is absolutely necessary and indispensable. (R. Paşca)

ビジネスから見る日本近現代史

　日本のビジネスの歴史は、近代日本の発展と密接に関わっています。近代工業発展の基盤となったのは、近世の問屋制家内工業や流通制度です。また明治時代には殖産興業政策の下で政府が工業化を主導し、外国から専門家や最新の技術を導入して、製糸業やその他経済の中心となる産業の近代化を図りました。

　近代日本経済は、政府と実業家との強い結びつきを特徴としています。実業家は政府から資金や払い下げを受け、新しい特権階級となりました。その中でも最も有名な実業家が渋沢栄一です。渋沢は株式会社や近代銀行制度を日本に導入し、数百もの多種多様な企業の設立や経営などに関わりました。

　ビジネス界において力を持つものとして財閥があります。同族支配による独占的企業集団で、第二次世界大戦が終わるまで日本の経済界に支配的な地位をもって君臨していました。その中でも四大財閥と言われるのが三菱、三井、住友、安田です。戦後、アメリカ占領下で財閥は解体されましたが、その後の冷戦におけるアメリカの方針変更により、その大部分は再結集しています。また、朝鮮戦争は日本の産業界に特需をもたらしました。

　1952年の日本の独立回復後、自由民主党は経済成長に力を入れ、経済重視の政策をとったため、多くの企業が発展しました。こうした企業の多くはエドワード・デミングのトータル・クオリティ・マネージメント（TQM）の影響を受けています。高い品質の製品を能率的に生産する手法で、日本の企業は自動車やカメラ・家電製造業において世界上位の地位を占めるようになります。日本経済は驚異的な成長を続け、20世紀後半には世界第2の経済大国となりました。しかし、1980年代後半にはバブル崩壊を迎え、長い不景気の時代に入りました。現在ではポップカルチャーも有力産業の1つとなっています。

（亀井ダイチ・アンドリュー）

Business and Modern Japanese History

Business has played a key role in the development of modern Japan. A foundation for modern industry was first laid during the early modern era, when cities developed as urban trade centers and proto-industrialization occurred. During the Meiii period, the government enthusiastically supported industrialization, drawing on foreign expertise and the latest technology to modernize the textile industry and other key sectors of the economy.

From the start, a defining characteristic of the modern Japanese economy was the strong relationship between the government and business leaders. Industrialists and entrepreneurs received government funds and even ranks in the new nobility. The most famous entrepreneur was Shibusawa Eiichi, who introduced joint stock corporations and modern banking to Japan as well as founding hundreds of corporations.

The dominant power in the business world was held by the *zaibatsu:* enormous family-owned conglomerates that controlled whole sectors of the Japanese economy until the end of the Second World War. The "Big Four" *zaibatsu* were Mitsubishi, Mitsui, Sumitomo, and Yasuda. After the war, the US Occupation authorities partly broke up the *zaibatsu*. However, they saw rebuilding Japanese industry as serving US interests in the Cold War. The Korean War was a boon to Japanese businesses.

Following the restoration of Japanese independence in 1952, the LDP government focused intently on economic development. Business-friendly policies encouraged the development of numerous companies and the application of the newest skills and technology. Many companies were inspired by W. Edwards Deming's "Total Quality Management" (TQM). With streamlined, efficient products, Japanese companies became leaders in manufacturing automobiles, cameras, and home appliances. The economy grew at a staggering pace, and by the last decades of the twentieth century was the second-largest in the world. However, during the late 1980s it experienced a major bubble. When it burst, the country entered a long period of recession. Today, pop culture has also become one of Japan's significant industries. (A. T. Kamei-Dyche)

❖日本の無形文化遺産❖

⑳ 山・鉾・屋台行事
Yama, Hoko, Yatai, float festivals in Japan

《巡行を中心とした祭礼行事》

地域社会の安泰や災厄防除(さいやく)を願い、「山・鉾・屋台」の巡行を中心とした青森県ほか17府県に亘る33の祭礼行事が無形文化遺産に登録されました。各地域の文化の粋をこらした飾り付けが特徴で、「山・鉾・屋台」は、木工・金工・漆・染織といった伝統的な工芸技術が維持され、自然環境を損なわない材料の利用等の工夫や努力によって何世紀にもわたり継承されてきました。

【登録年】2016年
【写　真】「佐原の山車行事」(提供：千葉県香取市)

■執筆者一覧 (50音順)

ウィンチェスター, マーク (WINCHESTER, Mark)
国立アイヌ民族博物館アソシエイトフェロー、前神田外語大学非常勤講師　専攻：アイヌ近現代史

神谷久覚 (KAMIYA, Hisaaki)
亜細亜大学経済学部経済学科講師、前神田外語大学非常勤講師　専攻：日本経済史・経営史

亀井ダイチ・アンドリュー (KAMEI-DYCHE, Andrew T.)
青山学院大学地球社会共生学部准教授、前神田外語大学非常勤講師　専攻：日本出版文化史

窪田高明 (KUBOTA, Komei)
神田外語大学名誉教授、神田外語大学学術顧問、日本研究所所長　専攻：倫理学・日本倫理思想史

土田宏成 (TSUCHIDA, Hiroshige)
聖心女子大学現代教養学部史学科教授、前神田外語大学教授・日本研究所所長　専攻：日本近現代史

パシュカ, ロマン (PAŞCA, Roman)
京都大学文学研究科助教、前神田外語大学日本研究所専任講師　専攻：日本思想史

町田明広 (MACHIDA, Akihiro)
神田外語大学外国語学部国際コミュニケーション学科准教授、日本研究所副所長　専攻：日本近現代史

松田清 (MATSUDA, Kiyoshi)
神田外語大学日本研究所客員教授、京都大学名誉教授　専攻：日本洋学史

吉田光宏 (YOSHIDA, Mitsuhiro)
神田外語大学外国語学部国際コミュニケーション学科准教授　専攻：文化人類学

吉村稔子 (YOSHIMURA, Toshiko)
神田外語大学外国語学部国際コミュニケーション学科教授　専攻：日本美術史